love *is* everywhere

nicole chini

Ark House Press
arkhousepress.com

© 2021 Nicole Chini

All rights reserved. Apart from any fair dealing for the purpose of study, research, criticism, or review, as permitted under the Copyright Act, no part may be reproduced by any process without written permission.

Unless otherwise stated, all Scriptures are taken from the New International Translation (Holy Bible. Copyright© 1996, 2004, 2007, 2013 by Tyndale House Foundation. Used by permission of Tyndale House Publishers Inc., Carol Stream, Illinois 60188. All rights reserved.)

Some names and identifying details have been changed to protect the privacy of individuals.

Cataloguing in Publication Data:
Title: Love Is Everywhere
ISBN: 978-0-6451031-7-5 (pbk)
Subjects: Christian Living;
Other Authors/Contributors: Chini, Nicole;

Design by initiateagency.com

"Some people put on clothes every morning. I put on love and wear it as the crown jewel it is."

To the woman who made me. To the woman whose life created my own. And to the woman whose death started it all. I love you. I thank you. This is for you. It was always for you.

Contents

To You The Reader xiii

PART ONE
SEEING LOVE

Seeing Love In Every Day 3
    Breakfast. Birds. And Ben. 4
    He Got Out Of The Truck 7
    Our Life Is Precious 10
    Superman 12
    Saturday Love 15
    Susan 16
    They Share The Same Tree 17
    Filling The Backseat and Heart 18
    Worcestershire Sauce 19

Seeing Love In Others 21
    Paws For A Drink 23
    The Blanket 25
    Love is What You Remember 27

Dodgem Love	30
The Every Day Little Things	32
The Man On The Motorcycle	35
I Smashed His Car And He Loved Me	38
The Red Capsicum	41
Lost Dog At Yoga	43
The Man With Bubbles	46

Seeing Love In Children 49

Love Behind The Action	51
Grandparents Day	53
Google	56
He Gave Him His Games	59
Julian And The Letter Box	62
The Perfect Shell	64
Lego	66

Seeing Love When It's Not Easy 69

I Love Sickness	71
The Dining Chairs	74
Naked	76
Releasing the Anger	80
You Can't Plan Life	84
Litter Bugs	87
I Imagine Their Deaths	90
Ashamed To Be Fat	93
Own Em!	97
No One Makes It Out Alive	100
Treasure The Moments	103

PART TWO
CHOOSING LOVE

Choosing To Love Others 109
- Olga 111
- "You Are Such A Good Driver." 114
- Lady In The Waiting Room 117
- Admit You're Wrong 121
- The Telemarketer 123
- Messy Rooms 125
- It Transforms You 128
- I Stopped 131
- The Icing Sugar 133
- Do I Ignore Or Say Hi? 136
- My Way - The Right Way? 139
- Wet Pants 142
- They Didn't Give Up 145
- The Hug Changed Everything 149
- Returning it Gifted Me 152

Choosing Love When It's Not Easy 155
- The Commitment 157
- The Kettle. The Toaster. The Morning. 158
- Piss Urine Wee. All that. 162
- Assumptions and Judgments In The Post Office 166
- The Jam Jars 169
- I Cleaned The Fitting Room 172
- Poo 176
- But I didn't 179
- Toothpaste 183
- Broken Glass 186
- The Kind Of Mummy I Want To Be 188

I Love You Both The Same	191
Hug Hater	193
The Drunk Guy	195

Choosing To Love You **199**
Out of Reach	201
Time Well Spent	203
Pronioa (pro. Noy. Ya)	206
Feet	209
Alone. Alone. Alone.	212
Days I fail	215
I Love You Nicole. I Love You.	218
He Bought Flowers	221
Saying No But Yes	224
Those Who Love You Through It	227
We Can Love Ourselves	230

PART THREE
BEING LOVE

Being Open To Love **235**
His Story. Our Story. All our Stories	236
I Made It A Habit	240
Hot Pink Lady	243
Kiwi Fruit	245
You Have An Amazing Voice	248
It's Not My Job!	251
The Shredded Pork Bun	254
The Letter	257
Withholding Love	260
Maths Class	263
Interrupted	266

    Making The Call 269
    I Accepted Him 272
    Brave and Bold.. 276
    Love Isn't A Currency 280
Being Love - How Others Do It..283
    Violin Love 285
    Please Let Me... 288
    Bring Back The Wave.. 292
    She Loves Her Husband.. 294
    He Sent Me A Text 296
    She Feeds Birds 298
    The Little Girl Who Gifted Me..................................... 301
    Dancing With The Fat Girl... 304
    Love Forgives 306
Being Love Is Simple 309
    Sitting on The Bus 311
    Loving By Seeing 314
    Post It Sandwiches 317
    I Was All Ears.. 320
    Bringing Light (and Wind!).. 322
    The Girl Who Sang... 325
    I Said Thank You 328
    Favourites... 331
    Return Or Complain 335
    My Son's Homework 339
    Eat Grapes. Bop Your Head. Be Happy 341

To You The Reader 345

To You The Reader

What's this book all about, you're probably thinking? Well love obviously. But who is the author behind the book, what's her story and why is she writing a book about love?

The author is me and my story. Well, that's for another time and another book! But this book you have in your hands is a part of that story.

My mother died far too early, well before I or even she was ready for. She was only 56 and I barely 30 and that's when everything changed. Nothing really 'out there' changed, but I did, because the moment she passed away I made a conscious decision there and then to live a full life, a life so full of love I wouldn't take a single day for granted!

I decided I would live life and appreciate every single day and moment I had on this planet. I vowed to myself to live the life she never got to live, appreciating it all and loving every moment. And in the 10 years since her passing I have.

Each day I'm given here I want to live with love. For me, for her and for every single person who has forgotten and needs reminding.

And this book you're reading is a result of my days learning to love; a journey which has me daily make the choice to look for and choose love, even in the smallest of ways. I see it in others and choose to see it when it's difficult, but mostly I simply just be it.

All the stories and experiences I have written about in this book were never written with the intention to some day be put into a book. But what I have come to realise in my journey with love is that love is to be shared and not kept hidden. Given and not held, acknowledged and not denied and something we must never feel too ashamed, embarrassed or frightened to share.

Which is why this book is in your hands.

I want you to see just how important, easy and simple it really is to love, feel love and be loved every single day.

You will notice I have included little 'practices' at the end of each story. I have done this with the hope to help inspire your own journey to loving every day. So if you are up for it, I challenge you to take on these daily practices and be the love this world is so desperately craving.

Because, you my dear, have the power to be this love.

Nicole x

Part One
Seeing Love

"You either see it or you don't"

Seeing Love In Every Day

"Every day can be a holiday to celebrate love"

I wish I could remember and tell you the first time I started seeing love everywhere. As though it were one huge moment where bang, all of a sudden, love became super obvious and popping up all over the place. Truth is. It didn't. It was never like that at all.

It just sort of developed over time. It developed the moment I made a conscious decision to start looking for love and the good in everything.

And it really is that simple!

And I guarantee you too can do it as easily as I can. And when you do, it will change your life forever in the most dramatic and love filled ways!

The following chapter contains stories and experiences about times I have witnessed love in every day simple moments. And I hope by sharing them here with you, you too will begin to see love everywhere in your every day. Because I assure you it's there, you just haven't noticed it yet…

Breakfast. Birds. And Ben.

Sometimes love is easy to see. Sometimes it isn't. Sometimes love comes in its obvious forms such as the sweet elderly lady baking cookies for the homeless. Or the man who devotes his entire weekend to looking after the kids while he sends his wife off for a massage and lunch with her girlfriends.

But then there are times when love is revealed in the most unique, spectacular and absolutely crazy of situations. Like this one morning I had whilst eating breakfast.

I share this story here with you all because it touched my heart so deeply and has remained with me ever since, even now many years later.

In a situation where I could have seen only death, destruction, and chaos I saw love rise, in the power of birds. Enjoy.

It all began one morning, just a normal everyday morning when I was sitting outside enjoying my breakfast in the sun.

At first I hadn't noticed him - Ben our cat. I was too busy admiring the array of gorgeous wild birds sitting on our lawn singing their little hearts out. It was the most magnificent sight!

As I sat there enjoying my breakfast admiring the birds, who had came out just to sing for me, unbeknownst to me, off in the distance, Ben, our cat crept closer, and closer.

Until all of a sudden out of nowhere he strikes!

In the corner of my eye, I see him dash across our lawn, followed by an almighty squeal, squawk, and one of the most horrible sounds I've ever heard. That's when I knew. Ben had a bird.

I jumped up so fast my bowl of cereal and all its contents flew absolutely everywhere and I ran to where Ben and the birds now were. And there it was, in Ben's mouth, a beautiful pink Galah.

I had to do something.

I looked around to see if I could find something I could pick up and throw at Ben in the hope he would release the bird from his mouth, but there was nothing. My next instinct was to kick our beloved cat Ben to free the bird. Yes, and this idea surprised me as much as it probably surprises you, I was actually going to kick him. My own cat.

I didn't.

But I was so desperate to free this terrified dying bird from the jaws of Ben, in that moment I was willing to do anything!

Yet, as soon as Ben saw me coming towards him he bolted with the squawking and terrified galah still in his mouth flapping like crazy. No way could I catch Ben now. He was gone. And this is where it gets amazing.

Because the next thing I know, completely out of nowhere, come four or five black and white magpies, all swooping in on Ben, attacking him from the sky. Then, in the distance I spotted three more birds on their way, white cockatoos this time. All of them came flying in towards Ben at mass speed, joining the five other birds in attacking him from above.

I had never seen anything like it.

Ben was surrounded and had no choice but to drop the pink galah and run. So he did and the pink galah was released from Ben's mouth and flew free.

All ten to fifteen of these different species of birds then flew themselves up onto the branches of trees surrounding our home and began, what I can only describe as a war chant!

It was a squawking and squealing, unlike anything I had ever heard before. Completely different to the beautiful serenade I had heard only moments earlier. This was victory. This was a celebration.

After the commotion had died down a little and my heart rate had gone back to normal, I returned to my little breakfast table out the front of our home and just sat there. Taking in all I had just witnessed. It was one of the most beautiful things I had seen in a long time.

All these birds, many who had come out of nowhere to help this dying captured bird. And a bird not even of its own kind or species!

The collection of birds I had seen out front of my home do not usually associate with each other or flock together, rather they often stay amongst their own species. But this day, out front of my place, they did.

Why?

Love.

And it reminded me how we, as humans, drop all race, colour and all our labels in the face of adversity and in life and death situations - 9/11, bushfires, earthquakes, massacres etc. During these times we are not our colour, race, sex or how much we earn. We are one. Part of this big earth family we call existence.

The birds on this morning demonstrated that sort of love. The love of being in a world together!

Practice:

Today as you go about your day, look out for love in nature. Can you see it?

Maybe you will see it, like I did, in birds? A mother bird cleaning or feeding her young baby?

Or maybe you see it in the way trees offer shelter from the sun or fruit for us to enjoy?

Or maybe it's the sun, which rises every day no matter what?

Or the bee, that flies by collecting pollen, so we can enjoy the delicious sweetness of honey?

Love is everywhere - and it isn't only in us, but in nature as well.

He Got Out Of The Truck

Love happens so simply, easily, and often so quickly in our every day it can be easy to miss.

As we go about our days, love is constantly happening all around us, and unless we notice it, it will simply pass by unnoticed.

There was one day I remember it didn't go unnoticed, because as I was out on an ordinary walk, I saw it.

Love.

Right there, in the action of a man who did something so seemingly simple and basic, it could have easily gone unnoticed.

But it didn't.

Because I saw it, and I saw him.

It was just a normal Tuesday morning, and I was out walking with my youngest son when I noticed a garbage truck doing the rounds. Not really a big deal I know, but when you have a young toddler with you who you are trying to entertain, seeing a great big huge truck is like the best thing ever.

So naturally we both stopped to admire the garbage truck. And my youngest son Gabe, well he was completely and utterly captivated by it. Score! A total win for both Gabe and mum.

We sat and watched this truck drive along the street collecting and emptying all the bins when I noticed something I normally wouldn't. The truck came to a complete stop and the driver got out.

Out of the truck.

This now had my attention, as the driver would normally never get out of the truck. Because these garbage trucks, in particular, are designed to automatically lift the bins from curb to truck. He paused only for the few moments it takes to completely empty the contents of the bin, before moving, and driving onto the next home.

I was curious.

So, being curious, I waited and continued watching as the driver stepped out of his truck and started walking towards the house he had stopped at.

Is he going to knock at the door? I thought to myself.

Does he know these people?

Why did he get out of the truck?

Then I saw it.

And I knew exactly why this man had gotten out of his truck. To grab their bin!

For whatever reason they had forgotten to place it by the curb that morning, the only home in the street that hadn't.

And yet, this man, a complete stranger to these people got out of his truck, walked down their driveway to their home, and grabbed their bin. He then wheeled it back to his truck where he physically lifted it up into the truck and emptied it by hand.

Once the bin was emptied he turned around and walked down the driveway, to where he had originally taken the bin from, and returned it. Next he jumped straight back into his truck, closed the door, and drove off continuing on his rounds.

And I just stood there.

Loving what I had witnessed and grateful to have seen it.

There are many reasons why the owners of this home may have forgotten to put their bins out. Perhaps they forgot as we all do at times, perhaps their bin wasn't full and didn't require emptying, or perhaps they weren't home and away on holidays.

Whatever the reason, it didn't matter. What mattered is what I witnessed this man do - a beautiful act of love.

Love honestly can be seen everywhere. And on this particular day, it was seen in a man's heart by his actions. A man who, by stopping his truck, knowing he didn't have to, did.

A man, who, knowing, he could have kept driving because the sooner all bins were cleared and emptied, the sooner his shift would end, and he could go home, didn't.

A man, who by stopping and getting out of the truck, did so not for himself, but to help another human, a human who will never be able to thank him for the kindness and love he had shown.

Love does that.

Love stops the truck and gets out, knowing there is no reward whatsoever in it except perhaps knowing you had helped someone. Someone you don't know and someone who can never thank you.

Practice:

Today practice is to like this man, gift another with love without them ever knowing. How you do this will be up to you, but I assure you there are countless ways you can do this.

You could pick up rubbish at a bus stop, a local park, or in your neighborhood. Or perhaps you wipe down a park bench seat, or bathroom sink. Or maybe you refill the coffee or milk at work so another person doesn't have to.

There are lots of little ways we can love others daily by helping them. And the best ways are the secret ones they never know about. The opportunities you spot to help and love another, not for yourself, but for them.

Because, love does that! It gives without expecting any returns, and it wants to do it every day.

Will you play a part?

Our Life Is Precious

Sometimes love can been seen at a time when you would least expect it. Like in a death. Or in another person's pain, grieving, or heartache. Which reminds me of a time when I saw love in such an occurrence by the roadside...

I was on my way to meeting a friend, running late as usual, when I drove past a car parked on the side of a freeway. I thought to myself what an odd place to pull over. Because it was. But I soon realised why they had.

There alongside the car stood a man and a woman at a small picket white cross, Both on their knees, both with their heads bowed, and the woman holding a bouquet of flowers. The woman was weeping and the man stood staring straight ahead with his arms wrapped around the woman.

I knew then exactly why they were there, and exactly why they had pulled over.

The man and woman had lost someone. Someone very close to them in a car accident at this very spot. Most likely even their child. Can you imagine?

For that moment I did.

I imagined losing one of my own children, but it was only just that. A thought. I had 'imagined' it. For many it's a reality.

I am not upset by these moments anymore. Quite the opposite - I am grateful for them.

I am grateful because they always bring me back. They bring me back to what I have and what's important. Love. Our love, and loving others with all we have, whilst they are still here with us alive.

In seeing this couple by the roadside I saw in their pain love. I saw the love we all hold for each other and those close to us. And I saw how quickly a life could be lost.

And it reminded me how each and every day is a gift and how things could always be much, much, worse.

Yet what do we focus on? What do we see?

Do we see love?

Or do we see the heartache and pain?

The day I passed the couple by the roadside, I saw only love. And although a life may have been lost, their love never will.

Practice:

Can you look back to a time in your own life, which may have been incredibly painful, yet love was present?

Perhaps you too lost someone close to you, or maybe a dear friend of yours went through incredible heartache, pain or an illness. Can you now see the love, which was present during this time?

The condolences from others, the meals cooked, cards sent. The help offered and received, the many phone calls, flowers, hugs, kisses, letters, all of it love and all given in different ways.

I promise you, if you take the time to look for it, you will find love in your pain. Because personally this is one of the places I have always felt it the strongest.

Superman

When you make the decision to start seeing love you soon see it everywhere. Even in places and things you never would have previously!

Like the day I saw a man dressed as superman. Where most people probably would have only seen a middle aged man dressed up as a super hero I saw only love. Here's why…

I was driving in my car one night on my way out for the evening when I saw a motorbike coming towards me in the opposite direction. Nothing unusual, I thought. Until … he got closer and I realised it was Superman!

No kidding. Superman. Cape, red underpants, blue tights and all! On a motorbike!

As he zoomed past, I noticed his cape blowing behind him in the wind. It was such a magnificent sight. And the scene looked just like in the movies when Superman was in full flight. I almost didn't believe my eyes at first and had to look back twice.

Now this wasn't on a highway or out in the middle of nowhere, but on the local main road, which leads into my suburb. The man was well into his 40's and by no means a child, yet here he was dressed in the full superman kit caboodle. And it wasn't even Halloween or any other occasion where you would dress up.

I loved it.

And am choosing to believe this man does this all the time, just for fun. That he dresses up as superman and goes out driving in local streets and towns, for no other reason than to make people smile as they pass him by.

As they pass him, people like myself look with awe, surprise and utter delight. And perhaps (even if only for a moment) believe in a little magic.

Even now many years since it happened, it has still remained with me because it was so unreal, so unexpected, and proved yet again how love really can be seen anywhere and at any time.

And on this day I saw it in the heart of a man who rode the suburbs dressed as superman for no other reason than to bring joy, love and happiness to the hearts of all who passed.

Practice:

Can you find love today in something unexpected, and see it in an unlikely way?

Can you open your heart up today to a little magic?

Perhaps you see it in a beautiful bird or butterfly, which happens to land right before you or on your path?

Or maybe the most unexpected and wonderful gift was sent to you?

Be open today, but mostly be on the lookout. Because I assure you, love truly is everywhere just waiting to be seen.

Sometimes love is so every day and simple we blink and can miss it. Or we see only what is in front of us rather than looking deeply into what is before us.

I can relate to many such times in my own life where for a moment, what I saw in front of me wasn't just an everyday circumstance, but love.

And in the following stories, I share with you examples of times when I or others saw love in such simple every day occurrences.

May the following five stories open you up to seeing love so simply in your own life, just as I have.

And I challenge you after reading the next five stories to look for ways in which love is already showing up right now in your own life. Because I assure you it is and as soon as you see it once, I promise you will continue seeing it, now and forever.

Because love is everywhere, it's simply waiting for you to find it. Will you?

Saturday Love

It was early one Saturday morning when, just like I had the previous three Saturdays I went to visit a dear elderly friend of mine in a nursing home.

I pulled up outside and was about to enter when I noticed a young man of around twenty, walk in with a bunch of flowers.

I watched him for a moment and was about to dismiss what I had seen, when I stopped and looked a little deeper into the moment. And what I saw was no longer simply a young man walking into a nursing home with flowers, but something more, something deeper, I saw love.

Now I know this sort of thing happens often. People walk into nursing homes all the time with bunches of flowers, so isn't it all love?

And what exactly makes this particular time so special?

Well, what made this so special to me was here was young man, a young man who could be doing absolutely anything at all on his Saturday morning. Things which most young guys would probably prefer to do on most weekends, yet he wasn't.

Instead he was up bright and early armed with a big beautiful bunch of flowers and was choosing to spend his time visiting an elderly old woman.

Love my friends. Love. That could only ever be, and is, love.

And that is exactly what I saw when I noticed this young man with flowers, and it could have so easily been missed. If I'm honest I've spent many years missing love, which was right before me. However, love changes people and it especially changes you when you start seeing it.

Love is infectious, it is contagious, and I assure you, when you see it once, you will begin to see it everywhere!

And you will realise love was always there.

Susan

There it was. Her name. Normally it means nothing. But on this day it meant something.

Because it was the third or fourth time her name had just 'appeared', and all in a matter of hours. It was now only at lunch when I saw her name written on the wall of my local coffee shop I finally stopped, took notice, and realised.

I realised this here wasn't just some freaky coincidence but was in fact her, my mum.

Call me crazy, but I like to believe it was her way of reminding me she is still with me and always is. I know it's something small and insignificant, like her name written in chalk on a board alongside a local coffee house. But to those who have lost someone, something as small as this can mean the world to you and completely change your day. It did mine that day.

Death may break the physical bond we have with our loved ones, but their love, the love, well nothing can or will ever take that way. Because love remains forever in our hearts and in the simple everyday reminders we see, such as a name written in chalk.

They Share The Same Tree

One morning I passed a tree full of birds and noticed another bird join the already overfull tree. And it had me thinking … birds all live together happily and share the same tree!

In this one single tree perched a variety of birds. So many different types of birds there were. I saw cockatoos, magpies, lorikeets, pigeons, and possibly a galah or two. And not one of those birds claimed this tree as their own or for only their particular species.

Nope they are all shared it together, in harmony.

And that is how I believe we all must live on this earth. Together. Sharing. And in harmony with one another.

This earth isn't mine, it isn't yours … it's ours! Just like the tree wasn't for the magpies, pigeons or the parrots, it was for all of them. And they knew it.

So much can be learned by the way birds live and love.

Filling The Backseat and Heart

I was driving home with my three boys all crammed in the backseat of the car, when something happened. For the first time I saw it all so differently.

I looked at them in the rear view mirror of my car, squabbling and fighting over whatever it is that brothers, when confined in such a small space of a car, fight about. And instead of becoming annoyed, irritated, or angry with them as I usually would, I felt extremely grateful.

Grateful to have them.

Grateful to have three beautiful boys who fill my car and my life.

And I realised in that moment I will never be lonely.

Knowing the boys will always be there, no matter where my life takes me, and however many people come in and out of my life, I will always have children. And I will always be their mum.

Love can be a funny thing at times. It enters when you least expect it, and in places and ways you'd never have imagined, like it did for me in our car on our drive home.

Yet the one thing love does every time, which is never unexpected, is change you. Because once it enters, no longer do you see anything else but love.

Love is in our days every day, it really is! But so often we don't allow it to be, or we close ourselves off to love by focusing on all that isn't love.

That day with my boys in the backseat I was open to it, I let in love. And instead of seeing three boys fighting and squabbling in the backseat of a car, I saw love.

Worcestershire Sauce

My partner Luke, like he does every Sunday morning, grabbed a bottle of Worcestershire sauce from the cupboard to have with his morning eggs. And as he poured this sauce on top of his eggs I was reminded of her - my mum.

I remembered how she once did this.

I remembered the first time I saw her sprinkle this sauce – the blackest of all black sauce, onto her scrambled eggs thinking she was crazy.

I remembered how disgusting I thought it was and telling her so.

Until I tried it myself.

And I remembered how not long after first moving in with Luke, he saw me do the same thing, giving me the exact same disgusted look I had given my mum all those years ago.

I remember the first time he tried it, like the first time I did, and loving it. Mum was onto something.

It's funny the things you remember. The things, which hold a special place in your heart long after someone you love passes.

I am not sure where my mum got the idea of mixing those two things together, eggs and Worcestershire sauce, maybe her own mother? But I do know it's little things like this that stay with you.

Never would I have thought or could ever have known how, as a young teenage girl watching my mother pour Worchester sauce onto her eggs, it would later some day become a cherished memory of her. A memory, which would keep her alive every time I saw someone else reach for the strange black condiment.

Life is full of these moments.

Those beautiful sweet moments and memories of those we love. And from someone who has lost someone dear to them, I can tell you that it is these moments you will soon come to cherish and love. And it's in these moments you see love.

Seeing Love In Others

"Love makes you the most beautiful person in the world. No matter what you look like."

One of my favourite places to see love is in others. And to be honest, it's the most common place I see it.

I remember when it first started happening – seeing love in others. And although I don't recall exactly what happened the very first time I saw it, I do recall what it did to me. The way it made me feel.

The beautiful warm, fuzzy, love feeling. The feeling the world is truly a great place to be and is filled with really amazing people. And it revealed to me something I had never ever noticed before…

How beautiful love makes you.

There is something so attractive and magnetic about those who walk in love. Those who go out of their way to help others, those who for a split moment do something so kind, so completely out of love it blows you away.

Then there are those whose love is more a long lasting type of love. A love, which has endured many years and trials, and perhaps it's only now, many years later, you see it in them.

Love.

It's Powerful.

And the following pages hold stories about times when I saw love in the hearts of those I know, those I love, and even those who only a few moments earlier, I did not know.

May these stories help you begin to start seeing all the love in your own life and in the lives of others.

Paws For A Drink

It was quite a few years ago now but I'll never forget it. And to this very day I still recall it each and every time I drive by their house.

I had witnessed an act of love so beautiful by people who once lived in this home. And of all places, it was right there on their front lawn.

Let me share with you more about a time I saw love on a stranger's front lawn.

Their home was around the corner from me. I would drive past it daily, as it was on my way to and from work, and also on my way home from picking the boys up from school, yet I never noticed it.

Until one summer I finally did, because something had caught my attention. Something, which was never there before. Something on their front lawn. A container of some sort along with a sign.

And I was curious. Real curious!

So, every time I drove past this home, I would strain my neck trying to read what was written on the sign. But I always drove by too quickly, and I was never quite able to read the writing. So the next day and day after that, I would try again, driving a little slower each time attempting, with all my might, to see what this container was and what the sign said.

One day, after a few weeks of doing this, I had had all I could take and decided to pull the car over and read the damn sign. Curiosity got the better of me!

And you'll never believe what it was and what it said.

On the sign, next to the container, which I noticed was full of water, it read;

'Paws for a drink' and was beautifully decorated with cute little paw prints.

I was so glad I had pulled over and saw it!

Because how great does it make you feel to know every day the owners of this place must go outside and refill this container with clean fresh water. Not for themselves, or even their own dogs, but for complete strangers. Strangers and their dogs, which happen to walk by their home on a hot summer's day, people, who they will never know or meet.

Why do they do this?

Love that's why! Love does this.

Don't ever underestimate the difference you can make in being kind. Being kind doesn't require you spend a lot of money, be incredibly talented, or give much of your time. It only requires you to open your heart and look for an opportunity to love someone.

Practice:

Today can you spot love in another person by their action? Or by them simply being kind?

Or better yet, can you be that person! Can you be someone today who is kind, open, warm, and loving to all you meet? And by doing so, you are the love this world needs.

Try it, make it a habit! Because not only will it make you feel great and others great, it's the very thing this world is craving.

The Blanket

Love. It isn't always 'I love you' spoken from the lips of our loved ones, or a passionate kiss, romantic date or time spent together. It can be something as simple as caring for another person's need.

For many years love to me was only the spoken word. The 'I love you' from my children and me to them, or from a husband to his wife, or girlfriend to her boyfriend. And when after years of never hearing these words from my loved ones, I began to feel so unloved.

Until I stopped and realised …

Love isn't words but an action, a feeling.

Love is something you do, and something you are. And I want to share with you all about the one time I saw love in my own partner, who had never spoken the words, but who has always shown it in his actions.

I had questioned for years whether Luke loved and cared about me. Because he had never said the words. But one day, I had the realisation that not everyone expresses love with words; some find it rather difficult to say. Yet this doesn't mean they do not love you, only they may have trouble expressing it.

It was only then, after this realisation, I began to see how Luke was loving me. One time, in particular, has always stood out. It was a Sunday evening and we had all sat down as a family to watch a movie together. It was a cold night and I had complained about it being so.

A few minutes after I had mentioned this, and even forgotten I had, Luke got up from the couch. He was gone only a minute or two when he returned with a blanket. A blanket just for me!

A blanket I had never asked for but so welcomed, and a blanket which he then proceeded to lay on me, tucking me in all cozy.

He may not say I love you, but it's moments like these I realise he does. And its moments like these, which remind me love has many languages.

Practice:

In what ways do you like to be loved?

Is it like me with words? Or is it by being gifted with a gift? Or perhaps someone doing something for you such as helping you with the dishes, cleaning out a cupboard, or carrying your groceries makes you feel loved? Or it may be spending time with someone such as going to the movies, shopping together, or going for a walk in the park?

There are so many different ways we can share and express our love and today's challenge is to do it differently than you usually would.

Maybe you normally share your love with words or gifts. Could you then today love someone by helping them? Offering to run an errand for them, take care of their children, or drive them to an appointment?

The list is endless because there are so many ways we can love others. Yet, most of us tend to stick to the one way. So I challenge you to mix it up a little and see if you can love someone a little differently than you would have done in the past.

Try it. It's so much fun! And please get back to me on how it all went.

Love is What You Remember

The following story is about a situation I'm sure many of us have had, or will find ourselves in. A time when seeing love is really difficult because the situation you are in is causing you to feel anything but love!

But don't lose hope, its possible!

Which is exactly why I am sharing this story.

Because this was a time when love certainly wasn't seen. Yet, I found it. I found it by remembering back to a time when I was in a similar situation and it was seen.

Traffic.

Love it or hate it. Resist it or curse it. Accept it or laugh through it all. Whatever you choose, it just is, and you can't avoid it. But you can always choose to look for ways in which love may be present.

Recently I was stuck in traffic, and I didn't see the love in it at all. But I was reminded of a time when I did…

I was only little, around the age of six or seven, when I witnessed an act of love so beautiful during one of the worst traffic jams I have ever experienced. Much worse than the one I had currently found myself sitting in.

We were living in Sydney at the time and were traveling back home from somewhere when there was a horrible fatal car accident. We did not know this at the time, of course, and it wasn't until we came to a complete standstill for over three hours we were told of the incident.

It's a wonder now, however looking back, I don't remember the wait at all, and neither do my parents.

Because do you want to know what it is about this time we remember? It was a kindness.

It was love wrapped up in the form of a sweet elderly dear old woman.

A woman we did not know who had come out of her home crossing lanes of standstill traffic to where we were all seated in our car waiting, carrying something in her arms. And it wasn't until she had almost reached our car we noticed what it was she was holding in her arms. A big container full of freshly baked cookies and cups of juice.

She had seen my parents, brother, sister and me all in the car, and I'm sure the many others waiting in cars in front and behind of us also. And out of her own free will and the goodness of her heart started baking biscuits to bring out to all of us. Fresh.

I was only young but I remember it all.

I remember my dad winding down the window and accepting these biscuits from a complete stranger. I remember my brother, baby sister and me all grabbing a biscuit and never having tasted a biscuit so good. And I remember the cold juice in plastic throw-away cups on a warm day.

Many years have passed (well over 30, to be exact), and I still remember this. It's all I remember about that time. I do know we were stuck in traffic for three hours that day someone informed me. But this isn't what I remember. I remember her. The sweet dear old woman and her biscuits.

A woman who has probably long since passed away, but her act of kindness never will. It will remain with me forever, and now even after reading this, possibly you.

The traffic jam I found myself in recently was only thirty five minutes, but in all honesty it was really only five. Because although the first five minutes I had spent impatient, angry and frustrated, the remaining half hour I was not.

The remaining half-hour was spent in love and gratitude, cherishing a moment from my past when a dear sweet old lady, whose name I'll never know, changed the lives of many by adding a little love to a situation.

Which, makes me conclude, love is present, even when it's not seen. You may need to search for it, look back on it later, or do as I did and let your heart take you back to a time it was. Even if only for a minute and in the form of a memory, love can always be found.

Practice:

The next time you find yourself stuck in traffic, or waiting unexpectedly longer than you had hoped. Return to love. Take yourself back to a time when love was present, sit there, sit in that love, bask in it, and let it wash over you until all you feel is love.

Dodgem Love

Love isn't always something grand, huge, or even obvious. It can sometimes be an act so small you'd almost miss it. Like, the day at the showground. However, on this day I didn't miss it, I caught it. I caught love in action. In the heart of man I did not know.

He was standing amongst many others with me that day in line at the Dodgem cars. I did not know him, had never seen him before, and to me, he was just one of the many who stood in line. And this is what makes his act of love so kind.

I was in line with my middle son Julian at the dodgems cars when I saw him, this man I did not know. It had come to Julian's turn and sadly he did not meet the height requirements to ride solo. At the time I wasn't able to ride with him (I was heavily pregnant), which meant we had not only wasted our time standing in the queue for over 10 minutes, but I now had one very disheartened and disappointed six-year-old.

That's when this man offered to ride with Julian. A complete stranger.

At first, I thought there was no way my son would want to ride with this middle-aged man he did not know. But the moment this man stepped forward with his offer, my son's face lit up and with a big beaming smile he said, … "Can I mum? Can I?"

I agreed to it and watched as they both jumped into the Dodgem car together. The music started, the dodgems powered up, and they were off. And I just stood there. Stood there watching as this man, a complete stranger who had forfeited his own solo ride to ride alongside my son, joke, laugh, and high five with Julian as they both rode together.

It almost brought me to tears that a complete stranger would do this for my son. It's one thing to offer to ride with someone, but to take it to the next level like this man had was something else!

To the many onlookers or others passing by, they would have thought they were father and son, or friends from long ago. No one would have ever have guessed only minutes earlier they had met for the first time.

And if that isn't some serious love in action then what is?

This man's act of kindness was something so much more than just a kindness. It was love. Bless this man and the many like him who daily show love in their selfless actions. May we all be more like these people.

Practice:

Can you today in some way (or in the coming days), offer an act of service so selfless, so kind and so completely unexpected like the man in my story did?

This sort of love isn't one we can plan or predict, only be open to and prepared for when an opportunity arises.

So be on the lookout!

Because I promise you, when you open yourself to the possibility of loving this way, opportunities WILL arise.

The Every Day Little Things

Love is most definitely an action. Yes. its words, thoughts, and feelings, but its most common expression is in the things we do. Our actions!

And every day little things that may seem insignificant and small at the time, when looking back on or differently at, is, in fact, love right there in action.

Like the one time when I saw love coming through the actions of a young man who worked in a supermarket. It wasn't anything special, or extraordinary he did, in fact it was so 'every day' you could have thought of it as nothing.

Yet because my eyes have been opened to seeing love everywhere, love is all I saw. And, as I share with you all about the time I saw love in such an ordinary every day action, my hope is maybe you too will recall a time when you saw something similar (love in an ordinary every day action), and realise in that moment, you were being loved.

He was a young man working at the supermarket, fresh out of school, or most likely probably still in school! A beautiful young man in the making he was this lad, who was about to go out of his way to love me a little.

It was the middle of the week when I found myself searching the entire freezer section at my local supermarket for Vienetta icecream. This icecream wasn't one we often have, in fact I don't think I had bought it before.

As we don't usually have this particular ice-cream I had absolutely no idea where it was. And after what felt like hours searching the entire dessert, icecream, and frozen goods section, I decided to ask the young employee I noticed nearby if he knew where it was.

He didn't.

But, he did however, direct me to the other end of the freezer section to where he thought it might have been. So off I went, heading over to where he had suggested, all the whilst doubting it would be there, as only moments earlier I had checked this exact spot.

And as predicted I still could not find this damn ice-cream anywhere. So what did I do?

I gave up. And purchased some fancy topping and plain vanilla ice-cream instead, which was much easier to locate, and then I walked away.

Just when I thought I had finally put the Vienetta icecream dilemma behind me and had almost completely forgotten about it I noticed in the distance the same young employee I had only spoken to earlier about the Vienetta icecream walking towards me. And there, in his hands, was one great big tub of the Vienetta icecream.

Immediately, after we spoke, he must have gone and searched one out for me. Now it might not sound like much, but the thing is, he didn't have to do this.

He didn't have to go and find it for me. And, after having found it, he certainly didn't have to pick it up and go searching the entire store for where I was now located. Which was in a completely different section of the supermarket aisles away.

But he did.

And he did it just for me.

What else can that be but love?

You may argue he is paid to do it. But is he? His job description is to stock and restock shelves, not chase customers around the store and do their shopping for them. No, that bit he took on himself out of the goodness of his own heart.

I've often said it's the little things others do that make us feel loved and appreciated, and it truly is. But do we ever take the time to notice every day the little ways others may love us?

I'm sure, if we all took the time to really think about it, we'd soon come to realise people are showing love to us every single day. We just aren't seeing it.

Seeing love in others is a choice you make, and a choice I promise will only ever bless you. Because it's only when you see love coming towards you that you can truly receive it.

Practice:

Be on the lookout today for love in action. Love in its simplest most every day form. This may sound easy, but believe me these sorts of every day love acts are the hardest to spot! Because sadly we simply let them pass by unnoticed or pass them off as 'nothing special'.

So, today, I challenge you to be on the lookout for the little everyday ways others may love you. And when you spot the receive them fully, as they were always intended – as love.

The Man On The Motorcycle

The story I'm about to share isn't my own. It's my mother's story. And it wasn't even her who shared it with me, but my father many years after she passed. The moment he told me I knew it had to be shared because it was one of the most beautiful acts of kindness and love I have ever heard.

And although my mother is no longer here to share this story, I know she would want it shared. As her way of thanking the men who went out of their way to love her …

My mother had been out shopping for most of the day with all us kids in tow. We were only very young at the time, and my sister was a newborn. So I can imagine it would have been one of those long, stressful and exhausting days.

Happy to finally have all of us in the car and go home, my mum began piling all the shopping bags into the boot of her car, and once finished, my mum shut the boot and drove off.

What my mother had forgotten to remember was while packing the car, she had placed her handbag onto the roof. And sadly, it wasn't one of the items she packed into her boot!

As you can probably guess, the handbag that was once on the roof of her car wouldn't be for much longer (especially if you've seen the way my mother drove).

So there she was driving down the road, music blaring, singing along to some rockin 80's tunes when she happened to look in her revision mirror. And when she did she noticed a group of bikers had come up close behind her and now surrounded her car. And they seemed to want her attention. They were flashing lights, waving, doing anything and everything they could to try and get her to pull over.

I can only imagine what she was thinking!

There she was, a young mother driving alone with her kids in her car, and now a group of men all on bikes, dressed in leather, were chasing her down, trying to get her to stop. And she wasn't going to. No way. She sped up, as she was sure they were 'chasing' her.

She kept driving as fast as she legally could trying to escape, when one of the men on the motorcycles speed up alongside her driver's window and held up his arm. And there, dangling from his arm was what appeared to be her handbag.

That's when she remembered and realised. She'd left it on the roof!

She immediately pulled over, and the men explained to my mother how they had seen her drive off down the road with a handbag on the roof of her car. And how only a few meters down the road it fell to the ground, so they raced to grab it. And that's when they began 'chasing' her.

I loved this story for so many reasons.

One: Because it's totally my mother.

Two: Because it was such a beautiful act of love and kindness.

And lastly and possibly most importantly, it shows us all how quick we are to judge.

My mother admitted she had judged those men based on the way they looked and the fact they were all part of a 'biker gang'. But the truth is she isn't the only one to fall victim to this sort of 'judging'. We all do it. We all judge.

But it just goes to show us doesn't it?

How love comes in many forms, and can often been seen in those you'd least expect!

So I say let's cast our judgments aside. And let's all be open to seeing love in others, especially those we'd least expect it from. Because love doesn't care who you are, how you're dressed, what you do, or what you look like. Love only wants us to be it.

Practice:

Today see if you can catch a moment where you are judging another. It may be a work colleague who you believe could work that little bit faster. Or the stranger you pass on the street and you 'judge' their outfit or the way they are parenting their children.

Or maybe it's a friend's choice in lunch. And the most sneaky kind … you may even be unconsciously judging yourself!

Whatever the way, whatever the judgment, catch it, let it go, and cast out some serious love instead.

Send the person you are judging love, wish them well, a great day, pray for them, or if you can bless them, because at the end of the day, do we really know what is going on in their lives?

No.

But we do know one thing for sure, we can love them not judge them!

I Smashed His Car And He Loved Me

Love.

Some people walk it, live it, and breathe it. And … some people don't.

And in the story I'm about to share I want to tell you all about one man. A man I met one day who I believe clearly walks lives and breathes love.

It was a dear friend's 70th birthday, and I was on my way to visit her when I decided to surprise her last minute with a bunch of helium balloons. So I stopped at a nearby specialised party store that sold the type of birthday balloon bouquet I was after.

I parked out the front of the store and my middle son Julian who was with me at the time, was in the backseat. I hopped out the car first and asked Julian to get out also, and we both went inside the shop together to purchase the balloon bouquet.

Leaving the store and returning back to our car, I noticed an older guy standing very close to my car. He was cleaning his own car parked next to mine with what appeared to be white cream and one super cool looking special cleaning cloth.

I thought to myself, 'Wow. He's keen', and how great it was he was being all particular with buffing and cleaning his car right there in the middle of a public car park. I didn't think anything of it until I went to help Julian into our car, and as the man stepped aside, I noticed our car door opened on to exactly where this man was cleaning his.

Which is when I realised.

This man wasn't cleaning and buffing his car, but removing marks made by my car onto his!

Julian, when getting out the car, must have ripped open his car door so fast it slammed straight into this man's car. At that time I hadn't noticed, but was now clearly evident by the silver-grey marks on his dark black convertible.

Yet this man didn't say anything. Not one word. He just stood aside and smiled as my son and I approached our car.

He didn't yell at me or tell me off for being so careless. He didn't throw abuse at me or blame me.

Nothing. Absolutely nothing!

He only looked up, smiled, and continued polishing and buffing the marks my car had made on his back passenger rear door.

I felt so awful I had to say something. So I asked him if he was cleaning marks on his car that were made by mine (even though I knew he was, I guess I was kind of hoping he wasn't!)

He didn't reply, just smiled at me and nodded.

I'm actually not sure if the man spoke English as he was an ethnic man. But I continued to apologise, again and again, telling him how sorry I was, and how I honestly did not realise my son had done this.

He continued to only smile, agree and nod at me. So I smiled back and got into my car as quickly as I could.

I wanted to get out of there fast and leave as I had no idea what to make of the whole thing or what to do next. I felt so incredibly embarrassed and bad about what had happened and was nervously awaiting and expecting an onslaught of abuse.

Yet there never was any, only smiles. And as I drove off, he even waved goodbye!

Did that really happen, I thought?

And who was this man?

I'll tell you who he was. A freaking saint!

A man so kind and beautiful he had only love and forgiveness in his heart. And I'll never forget him. Ever.

Practice:

Next time someone offends you or accidentally ruins your day or spoils something you made or own. Can you, like this man had, let it all go, forgive them, and not say a single word about it?

It will be tempting to pull the person up and expect an apology, or for the item to be replaced, or even for them to rectify their mistake. But could you for the moment consider perhaps this person did not intend to offend you, ruin your day, or do whatever it is they did to upset you?

Perhaps they didn't know any better, or were only doing the best they could in the situation.

And peace, love and forgivness is always so much better than allowing anger, bitterness and unforgiveness to brew in your heart and ruin relationships.

Choose love by choosing to let go and forgive. Forgiving others and treating them the way you would want to be treated in the same situation.

The Red Capsicum

You are going to keep hearing me say this, but only because it's true. Love really is in the simple every day things you and I do for others daily.

And although most of the time we wouldn't think much of it, and perhaps not even notice the love, it's there.

And once you start seeing it I guarantee you'll begin to see it almost everywhere!

That's the only way I can explain how I saw love in a red capsicum.

Well it wasn't in the red capsicum itself I saw love, but in the lady who picked it up.

I doubt she would have even have thought what she did was love. But it was. Because love is totally awesome like that!

And once you start noticing love, you'll honestly see it everywhere. In others, in yourself, and in everything! Including red capsicums.

I had just finished grocery shopping one evening and upon leaving the store, a red capsicum fell out of one of the many bags I was carrying. I didn't realise at the time until I heard a lady from behind me calling out and running towards me.

I turned around and noticed she had a great big red capsicum in one her hands and was waving it in the air. As she approached me, she said, "Is this yours?" "It fell out of one of your bags."

I realised it must have been mine as I did buy a capsicum, and I was the only one near her at the time. I took the red capsicum from her hands and thanked her, and she returned to the cashier where her own groceries were currently being checked out.

And that's when I saw it. The love.

This lady didn't have to do what she did that night - she could have instead noticed my red capsicum fall from my bag and ignored it, keeping to herself. But she didn't. She took the time to stop, leave what she was doing and walk over to my capsicum and bend down and pick it up. Then after picking up my capsicum, she chased me down, calling out after me.

And I'm grateful she did.

Love is everywhere. It's in other's kindnesses, and it's in the actions we do every day from our heart. This was only a small act and one this lady will probably never think of again, but it made a difference. A difference to me!

Had it not been for her when I went to make the meal I planned later in the week with the red capsicum, I would have realised I didn't have one. And then been left with two choices, leaving it out, and running the risk of ruining the dish or, spend more money (and time) racing down to the shops quickly to buy another.

None of this happened, all because of her, her kindness, and her love.

Don't ever doubt the difference your love can make. Even something as small as picking up a dropped red capsicum for another person, can make all the difference in the world.

Practice:

Be on the lookout today for opportunities to love others in simple ways. You may already be doing these acts of love daily without even realising you are doing them! But today, see if you can intentionally notice the way you love others by simply helping make their life easier in some way.

Lost Dog At Yoga

Love isn't only seen in others, but can also be seen working through others. And to be honest, it is one of my most favourite ways to see love.

There is one particular time in my life I will never forget. A time where I saw this type of love. A love which worked through the lives of two people who did not know each other, yet were brought together by what could only be described as love.

And I share this story to remind us all how truly magical life can be.

It happened once in a yoga class. I remember it like it was yesterday. It was a Wednesday night in a class held in a small village town. The teacher lived locally, as did many of the students from the class.

As we were about to begin our class warm up the teacher made small talk, asking one gentleman in the class (a local), if the dog he had found earlier during the week had been reunited with it owners. He wasn't sure.

The gentleman and the yoga teacher continued to discuss this, and I was listening. A trait I've always had - listening to other people's conversations and being nosy. But this day, it paid off!

I continued listening as they discussed how the storms earlier in the week must have scared this poor dog, and they both agreed this is most likely what caused the dog to have ended up out of his yard and into the man's property.

The man continued to tell how he had knocked on everyone's door in town that evening trying to locate his owner. He wasn't successful. No one seemed to know who this dog belonged to.

As my yoga teacher was setting up to begin the class she asked this man one final question. If he knew what ended up happening to the dog?

He told her the pound had come for the dog and found the owners. The man also expressed how curious he was about where this dog had originally come from and who the owners were. But due to privacy reasons, the pound could not release this information, only say someone had collected the dog.

This is where it gets miraculous. And this is where life and love worked their magic...

A lady standing near this gentleman must have also been listening into this conversation, as all of a sudden she blurts out ...

"Honey!"

"Was it my Honey?"

She then went on to tell how her dog had run away the week before and they found her at the pound. Someone had brought her in.

The man and this woman looked at each other from across the room. Surely it couldn't be? This lady lived miles away; it couldn't be the same dog. Was it just a coincidence?

The lady then asked this man if the dog he had found and taken to the pound was a Chihuahua wearing a pink sparkly collar. The man said it was and it was soon realized this was the same dog. Her Honey!

There he was, the man who had found her dog standing in her yoga class. A yoga class she never usually goes to but decided to join a friend at the very last minute.

What are the chances?

It was such a beautiful thing to witness and is something I will never forget. Because I believe life is full of moments such as these.

Moments where things so miraculous happen that it can only ever be love. And it has me convinced more than ever life will always have us be exactly where we need to be.

And even more miraculous was both this man and the women were recently single. I like to believe more was at work here that day than just reuniting a lost dog with her owner. I like to believe it was love bringing two people together who were destined to be together all along.

I never will know how the story ended, but that's the beauty of love. We never do know when or where it will turn up, only that it always does.

Practice:

Think back over your own life. Can you recall a time in your own life where something magical occurred? Some miraculous uncanny, and unlikely event which happened.

Can you now see how love was evident here and what it brought you?
New friendship?
A close call or life saving situation?
Or a lead, which took you in a completely different direction in life?
Love often appears in the most unexpected, miraculous ways, and more often than not, delivered by complete strangers.

The Man With Bubbles

Sometimes we will miss out on seeing love in others because we are too quick to assume it's not.

We won't ask questions. We won't take the time to look at a situation a little closer and see it all differently. We simply just assume.

I've been guilty of this many times, and I remember one time I was almost guilty of doing it again, until I didn't.

Instead, I asked, opened myself up, and in return, so did this man. I discovered a man who wasn't just a man 'doing his job' and being paid to do it, but something so much more.

He was love.

Love, I must admit I would never have seen if I hadn't looked a little deeper.

Love is everywhere, it really is. It's only sometimes hidden underneath our own perceptions and judgments of what is right before us.

A few summers ago I was meeting a friend in the city with my youngest son Gabe. The city was holding a free event with face painting, free gelato, and even free jumping castles for the kids. And. A man with bubbles!

Not just any bubbles mind you, but big gigantic huge massive ones. Ones you could just about fit into.

The man I assumed was all a part of the morning's events and had been hired by the organizers to be there. Until I noticed his set up - an old falling apart bike with two big bottles of detergent strapped to either side with belts.

Not proper bike belts either, but the ones you use to hold up your pants! You know, with loopholes, a buckle and all.

Not very professional I thought …

Which is probably what prompted me to ask him about the company he worked for. Because I wouldn't work for such a run down company! And that's when he told me.

He told me he does this every weekend and has done for years.

Not for money, not for work, but for the pure joy it brings the children.

He explained to me how it wasn't a business, never has been, nor will it ever be. He simply does it for the pure joy and fun it brings to him and the children he meets. And he added all coming out of his own expenses and pension.

He told me how he will often walk up and down laneways and open spaces in the city or city parks searching for the perfect place to begin his bubble blowing madness (the bubbles are seriously huge!).

On the particular morning I saw him he explained how when he noticed a huge gathering of people, children, icecream, and jumping castles, he knew it would be the perfect spot to set up and showcase his bubbles.

As he told me all this I just stood there. Shocked. Overwhelmed with gratitude and love for what this man does.

From the goodness of his own heart, this man spends his days out in the hot summer sun blowing bubbles to bring children joy. And all at his own expense, never once asking for anything in return or placing down an upturned hat to collect donations and offerings.

And here I was thinking the event had hired him!

I thought he was only there because he had to be because he wanted a bit of extra cash. Little did I know (and never would have had I not asked) this wasn't a once-off kind act. But a lifestyle he had been living and pursuing for years.

What a man!
And what led him to this?
Love.
What else could it be?
Seriously. What else?
It isn't money, recognition, or because he feels he has to. It's love.

What else would have you go to the effort every day of filling up huge big 10 litre containers of bubble mixture, strapping them to a bike, and then carting them along with bubble wands and all sorts of other equipment, for goodness knows how far or long?

Love.

That's what.

I'm not sure what anyone else saw that day - maybe they saw just an old man blowing bubbles. But that day, all I saw was love. And all because I had asked and didn't assume.

Practice:

Can you see love in a situation you normally wouldn't?

Can you look past your own judgements and assumptions and look a little deeper for the love?

Now I admit, love won't always be there. Because sometimes, it isn't. But nine times out of ten, love is. And when you find it, I assure you, you will be the one blessed by it.

Seeing Love In Children

> *"I love the creativity of children. The way they can sit down to a bunch of lego and turn it into something magnificent. When all I see is individual lego blocks, they see creations waiting to happen."*

Children have such a great view on life, don't they?

And the above quote about lego was something I had written about my own children a few years ago when they went through that 'lego' phase all kids seem to go through. Lots of fun, and … lots of cleaning up!

Another thing I love about children is how they view life so openly and with open hearts.

Love is always much more evident in their lives than it is with our own, as adults. It's as though their sweet dear little hearts are braver and less guarded than ours when it comes to love. And I love that.

I also believe this is the only way to live. Yet sadly, many of us don't. Including me.

However I am committed to living each day more and more the way children do.

With a heart so wide open to love I am willing to be it, share it, and to live it every single day of my life.

And on the following pages I share stories about times I saw love so beautifully in my own children, and also in others.

May these stories inspire us all to live more the way children do.

Love Behind The Action

To some people love is being showered with gifts, for others it may be hugs, kisses or attention. And then there are those who, love for them, is simply your time or telling them how much you love them.

And yes, it's all love.

But what I find most common of love is how it is always the 'thought' and 'intention' behind the action which makes it love.

And it reminds me of one time I saw love this way because it wasn't what my son did or gave me exactly, but his love behind it. Because at the end of the day, the only reason he was doing it was for love. And if we all made love the only reason we ever did anything, what a beautiful world we would live in.

As I walked past my boys, I overhead my middle son Julian say to his brother…

"I'm making daddy his very own house on Minecraft, just for him, because it's his birthday!"

Bless that child and his heart.

He has nothing to gift his father or the money to buy something even if he'd wanted to. Yet the one thing he did have was a passion (read: almost obsession) with the online game of Minecraft at the time.

So there my sweet son was spending hours, days, possibly even a week building his father, his very own house in his online gaming world of Minecraft.

Now Luke, in all honesty, at the time probably didn't think too much of it, but I hope he saw what I saw that day.

Love.

Love in a little boy who, wanting to give, yet with nothing at all to give and no money to do so, gave the only thing he could. Himself. Using the only prized possession he had, his favourite game.

Love. It doesn't cost a cent. It honestly doesn't. It costs only our time and a little piece of our hearts wrapped up and presented in whatever way it can.

And children, they do that best.

Practice:

Can you love someone today the way my son had his father, with your time? Loving them with the most valuable thing you could ever give them, you.

Grandparents Day

I love kindness because to me kindness is love in action, and every time I see it in others it completely warms my heart.

I witness it most in children.

They seem to naturally have the ability to be kind and loving in almost everything they do!

Yet somewhere along the way this kindness, this effortless giving of love, seems to not come so naturally. Well, at least for me, it doesn't. I tend to 'think' about and 'rationalize' my acts of kindness and love.

Whereas children don't even give it a second thought. They simply just act straight from the purity of their own hearts.

I have a great example of this kind of selfless giving and love. And I want to share this story with you to bless your hearts as much as it did mine. And perhaps even opening it up today to share all the love it holds.

My son Hugh was in kindergarten at the time, and it was Grandparents Day. A day the school holds every year where grandparents go to spend the day at school with their grandchildren.

Although not a grandparent, I accompanied my mother-in-law to school that day as Hugh had chosen Luke's mum (his Nanny) to spend the day with him. It was a fun morning, and it was time for children to have their morning tea break.

One girl in Hugh's class became upset and started to cry. She was sitting all by herself and, noticing her cry, walked up to her and sat down beside her. I asked her if she was ok and what was wrong. She told me she was upset because her grandma didn't turn up and all the other kids had their grandparents.

Another girl in her class had noticed this young girl I was sitting next to and how upset she was. This girl then got up from where she was sitting and eating and walked over to us both. She didn't say a word at first, only handed the upset young girl a pretty little bag decorated with ribbon.

I knew exactly what this bag was.

I had seen them myself for sale earlier in the day. They were bags filled with special handmade chocolates and treats which only grandparents could purchase for their grandchildren.

The young girl looked up at this girl, who now stood in front of her with the gift bag, and began to smile and accepted the gift.

The little girl who had given the bag said to her, "My grandma bought this for me, but you can have mine. I noticed everyone has one but you, and I'd like you to have mine."

How beautiful is that!

And how many of us would have done this?

How many of us would have given away something we wanted for ourselves to another?

And how many of us would have given it away knowing we would then have to go without?

Love.

Love does that.

Pure selfless love. And a lovewhich is so often found in the hearts of children. My only hope is they never lose it.

Practice:

Think of something you own and treasure; something which you have that another person does not.

Could you possibly gift this to them and go without?

Gifting them for no other reason than to love them and share with them something you hold dear and love, and now want them too?

Google

I'll never forget the following story I'm about to share with you. It is one that has stayed with me for many years and will continue to because it was the first time I saw true unconditional love from my eldest son towards his brother.

Most children, when young, are superficial and selfish, which is perfectly ok and normal. Because when children are young it's often hard for them to see outside of themselves and into the lives of others.

Then there are moments like the time I'm about to share with you, when a child can surprise you with an act of love which is so beyond their years and even your own.

Children, may we never underestimate them and their capacity to love.

My boys were only young at the time. My eldest was six, and his younger brother Julian only four. Julian was in tears on this one particular morning because of the pain he was experiencing in his belly. He had been going to the toilet all morning and told me he had 'runny poos' and a belly ache.

At some point his older brother Hugh must have heard Julian mention this, which was hard not to. Because of the tears, crying, and commotion it was now causing to the entire household.

Amongst all this I was trying to go about the usual morning routine for the day. Tidying up the kitchen, getting breakfast ready, school lunches etc, when I noticed my eldest son Hugh on the Internet.

I was curious.

He was only five at the time and at this age had only ever used the computer for You Tube clips, roblox and online maths games.

So when I walked passed him and noticed Google's home page on the screen I was concerned.

What was he searching I thought...?

And how does he even know Google?

I walked up to where I could get a better view of the screen and read what he was searching in the search bar, fearing the worst. Because as a parent Google can unintentionally open your children to a world of things their eyes and hearts are not yet ready for.

However I had absolutely no need to worry. Because there it was. Right there in the search bar. Two words. Fixing and diarrhea.

Hugh must have heard me mention to his brother that his runny poo's where something called diarrhea and then ran off to search it up on the Internet to help his brother.

No one asked him to do this or expected him to; he was after all barely six years old. Yet there he was, looking up ways to help his little brother and stop the pain.

He could have been using the little time he has on the computer in the mornings doing what he loves most, playing online games. But no, instead, he was using this time to research help for his younger brother.

And my oh my did that touch my heart!

It was so compassionate, so loving, and showed me that morning despite their fighting and Hugh's selfish ways, he does care deeply for his brother.

Love.

It isn't something that is learnt or taught. But embodied and birthed in an open and willing heart. And children's hearts especially are always open.

Like my five year old when he saw his little brother in pain, and without a word from anyone or even asking if it was ok, took it into his own hands to research up and cure his little brother.

Only love would do that.

Practice:

Today when you go about your day, I challenge you to notice children particularly. Can you see and witness their open and vulnerable hearts in action?

Can you see how a child so openly loves, receiving and giving love without even questioning it?

Take notice and if you can, see if you can do the same. Open your heart up completely to love and all it has to offer.

He Gave Him His Games

Selfless giving. Children do it best. Yet at the same time, they don't. I can recall many times when my young boys would refuse to give the other a piece of their chocolate, or share a toy. Which is what makes this story so beautiful.

It's about a time when my eldest son, a son if I had to pick any out of all three, was the least likely to do this sort of thing, did.

He is beautiful my eldest, but can also be a little possessive and self-absorbed (read selfish). So to see him do what he did that day can only be described as love.

It's a powerful thing love.

And I don't care who you are, what you may have once done, or even if you believe you could never be loving, I am here to tell you all it's possible. Because love moves through us all. We only need to let it and open ourselves to it.

There was a younger man in my dear friend Olga's nursing home called Gordon. I didn't know too much about Gordon except I'd see him every time I visited Olga. He was in a wheelchair, in his late 40's, and seemed very 'normal', a word I would prefer not to use, but compared to the many others who lived in the home, he seemed very able.

The nursing home had an Xbox and Gordon was the only person I had ever seen playing it. In fact, it may have even be his. I'm not sure. And every time I saw him playing, it was always the same game, a sporting game of tennis.

We also owned an Xbox at the time, well Hugh did. It was his.

So one afternoon I thought I'd ask Hugh if he had any games he no longer plays or would be willing to give up and give to Gordon. I knew it was a long shot and my expectations were not high. Hugh didn't own many games himself and absolutely loved the Xbox. He would play it every afternoon.

Hugh had never met Gordon, but he had seen him playing the tennis game on the odd occasion he came with me to visit Olga.

After 10 minutes of some serious consideration, Hugh came back to me with two games. Two! The boy only owned a total of five games. And I've forgotten to mention here that Hugh was only very young at the time. A time where selfishness rules.

I was so proud of him, I expected none and was ok with that. I had really only asked as a way of showing him how blessed we are to own what we own and have what we have when others in this world have far less.

Yet the best part of this was the games he gave me. He gave me his two favourites. The two games he played the most.

Did I end up giving them to Gordon that day? I'm not sure. I honestly think I may have let Hugh keep those two - they were, after all, his absolute favorites.

But the true gift in all this was the love. The love I saw in Hugh when he offered up his two most prized processions to a man he did not know. How many of us would do that?

Practice:

This one may challenge you a little, and you may even skip straight on past this once you read it. But if you can, see if you can take on the challenge like I once did and do this.

Find something you own that you dearly love and treasure. Maybe it is something you use regularly or maybe it's something you no longer use, but dearly treasure.

Could you possibly gift this to someone who would value it more than you do right now, or perhaps needs it more?

An example in my own life would be a pair of earrings I once owned and so dearly loved. I have many I love, but this pair in particular, I really admired. A lady I know every time she saw me wearing them complimented me and mentioned how much she loves them, and she would ask where I bought them. They were no longer for sale; I had the only pair.

So I gave them to her.

Why?

Because I had worn them many times and had so many other pairs of beautiful earrings at home, and it was her time now to shine and be seen in them. And maybe, just maybe, someday she too will pass them on?

Love gives.

It never hoards, keeps or withholds, only ever gives.

Can you give today?

Julian And The Letter Box

Love. Sometimes it just knocks you over the head and gives you the wake up call you need.

Love will always bear gifts, always. Yet sometimes the gift may not be entirely what you expect. It can be more of a wake up call. Like the time I found the wake up call in my middle son's love.

His actions and his love on this day was just the reality check I needed.

Maybe you can relate …

It was a morning like any other, yet for some reason, I found myself particularly stressed. You know the days, days where every little thing just seems to tick you off, and you find yourself getting agitated over every little thing.

I was not my best on this particular morning, and my poor son had himself one cranky mumma, who sadly was taking it all out on him.

In the midst of my crankiness I sent my son Julian out to the letterbox to check the mail. And to be honest, I really just wanted him away from me for a few moments.

I needed a break and really didn't want to take my bad cranky mood out on him as I had been for the past few hours. So I sent him outside.

Not long after I sent him out to the letterbox he was back again. But he had something. I could see it, there in his hand behind his back. It was a flower.

He walked straight up to me with a huge grin on his face and said as he pulled the flower from out behind his back, "Mum I picked this just for you."

It almost made me cry.

There he was, my son, the son who only moments earlier I was yelling at in the kitchen, standing there with a flower picked just for me. A flower which he would have went searching for when I sent him to the letterbox to get away from me.

Wake up call or what?

Who was the mature one here? Who was being the most loving, caring, compassionate and kind?

It clearly wasn't me.

Julian showed me that day what true love is all about.

Forgiveness.

And loving others when they shut you out, close down, or send you away to a letterbox.

And when they come back you hold only love for them. As my son did that day in the form of a flower.

Pratice:

Is there someone you can forgive today? And not only forgive but love?

In the coming days lookout for opportunities to love others when they are aren't their best, or so loving to you.

Love is the most powerful force there is, and to love someone, especially when they aren't loving towards you, is one of the most incredible things you could ever do.

The Perfect Shell

Children will often see love in places we struggle to, and at the same time unintentionally give us such deep insightful life lessons.

Like this one time, a time I will never forget when walking along a beach with my young son.

Where I saw brokenness and no use, he saw hope. He saw love when all I saw were broken, no good damaged shells.

Let me explain more.

I was walking on the beach one summer with my middle son Julian. We were searching for seashells as Julian had wanted to take some shells home to show and share with his preschool the following day. However, due to the recent wild weather, the beach was eroded, and most of the shells were shattered and broken.

As Julian kept picking up these broken pieces of shell to take home, I kept telling him to put them back, saying "No. Not that one. Let's find a better one, one that isn't broken."

Which was almost impossible as every shell had either a mark, hole, or was snapped in half. We continued searching until I realized the absurdity in it.

What is the perfect shell?

There is no such thing as a perfect shell!

And that's when it happened. Two big life lessons and epiphanies.

That I (like I'm sure many others) strive for perfection. And second, and probably the biggest one, that we as people are just like those shells.

All different, each with our own war wounds, breaks, and tears, yet still perfect in our own way.

Julian taught me that day to see beauty in the broken. And he taught me just because a shell is broken doesn't make it any less of a shell or any less beautiful. It still deserves to be admired and shown. And just because something isn't completely whole and perfect, it is still worthy.

And I believe this is exactly what love sees. Beauty in the broken. Hope in the hopeless. And shells worth keeping and showing off to others.

From then on I let him collect whatever shells his heart wanted him to choose. And I stopped searching for the perfect shell. Because I realised each and every shell already was.

Practice:

Can you, for today, see beauty in the broken?

Can you see beauty in something you would usually class as 'unbeautiful'?

It may be an overcast day, you may have dirty windows, or a stain covered top. It may be that horrible wart you've had all your life, or a neighbor's hideous choice in curtains.

Could you find beauty in these things?

Or how about broken things? Things you class as broken and no longer of use? Can you see the beauty in these? Love, which was once held by them and continues to?

This practice may require some searching and a little effort on your part, as it doesn't come naturally to us to see the beauty in the broken and beauty in the 'not so beautiful'. But I assure you it is, like all things when done in love, possible.

Lego

They were aged seven and five at the time. I'll never forget it. Never forget the hours they had spent on its creation, and the three seconds it took me to demolish it.

They were so forgiving. So full of compassion. So full of love. And expressed it all in one small simple sentence.

Let me take you quickly back to that day and time …

There had been a terrible accident, catastrophic in fact. Well, ok, catastrophic is a bit dramatic and a complete exaggeration. Because for me, it wasn't. But for a certain two young boys, I knew it would be.

I expected the worse. Tears, anger, tantrums, and hours of uproar for what I had just done. But there was none. Only love. Only one sentence, "It's ok, mummy, we aren't mad at you, we still love you," and all said whilst running up to give me one great big bear hug.

I had just told them there had been a terrible accident and led them both to their Lego plane creation, which now lay in a thousand pieces on the floor. A plane they had spent the entire morning constructing.

A plane they were so proud of and wanted to keep to show others. A plane I had so carelessly a few minutes earlier picked up, dropped, and smashed.

Yet when I led them to the scene of the crime, did they cry, scream, yell, or blame me?

No.

All they said was:

"It's ok, mummy. We aren't mad at you - we still love you."

Ah, those boys. My sweet darling beautiful boys who remind me daily how to love and forgive, always, no matter what.

Children. They really do embody love.

Practice:

Today make it your mission to love hard. To love everyone and everything openly, widely, and with full compassion and a truckload of enthusiasm!

Be like my boys had so beautifully demonstrated to me - wide open and full of love.

Seeing Love When It's Not Easy

"When I was a boy and would see scary things in the news, my mother would say to me, 'Look for the helpers. You will always find people who are helping'." - Fred Rogers

Love is all wonderful and good when life is good. But when it's not, when things are down, and life is hard, that's when seeing love seems almost impossible to do!

But it isn't. It's possible!

Because love is still there. It's always there.

Love doesn't vacate and vanish, the moment life gets tricky, and you're having a bad day. I believe it is almost the opposite and it's during these times love is with us more. Calling, waiting, yearning to be seen!

Love never leaves, and it certainly never leaves on someone's deathbed. In fact, this is one of the places I have seen love most - in those hard and difficult moments, the times when it's hardest to see.

Because in those times, the times when we need love most, I look for it.

And in the following stories, I share about times when seeing love wasn't easy or obvious. Times where I had to seek it out and look for it. And every time I did, I found it. Found the love and then felt the love.

Because love does that!

It transforms you. Every single time. It's why I love, love, so much.

I've said it before, but I'll say it again… love totally rocks!

So no matter where you are right now or how grim your circumstances may be, look for love. Because I promise you it's there. It's always there. It just sometimes takes us a little longer to see.

I Love Sickness

One of the most difficult times to see love or even feel love is when you are sick.

Sickness is one of those times in our life which seems to not have anything good about it at all. However I love when sickness strikes. I honestly do. Not the sickness itself but what it offers me.

Ever since I started seeing love in everything, I can now see sickness the same way - with love. And this is exactly what I am sharing with you all.

Because up until recently, I was never able to see any love in sickness at all. Now, whenever sickness is upon me I see it as a gift, and I receive the love it has for me.

By sharing my view of the love I found in sickness, I hope it will help you will help you to discover love in your own lives and in those around you.

I use to hate sickness. the way it made me feel, hated the way it would throw everything I had planned for the day, week, or weeks into chaos. And I hated how it always left me feeling unloved and alone in the world.

Until recently.

When I decided enough was enough!

And I made the decision to search out and find the love in sickness.

Because if what I say is correct, and what I believe to be true is true, then love has to be there! Even in horrible sicknesses, which plagued half my family and me.

Surprisingly it didn't take long to find the love either. Only a little shift in perspective! I started by thinking about what gifts the sickness I was experiencing was gifting me.

What is this sickness bringing me, which is 'good'? I asked myself.

And what would result from this sickness that otherwise wouldn't if I were well and not sick?

And this is what I discovered.

Sickness makes you stop.

Sickness makes you take it easy, and gives you no choice but to rest.

And it miraculously makes the things, which seemed so important yesterday no longer seem so important. Because the only thing necessary to you right now is getting better and loving you!

Whenever I'm sick, I know what it means. It means it's time for me to love me. Time to nurture and look after me the same way I would if any of my three boys were unwell. And the time to do nothing, except give myself all the love, compassion, and kindness I need.

And as tempting as it is to complain or feel sorry for myself, I don't. I no longer travel down the road of self-pity because after many years and experience of doing this, it never works. It only makes me feel worse.

Yet what does make me feel good is loving me and caring for myself! But sadly, for many of us, we are never shown or taught how to do this. And I hope and pray that someday sickness will be viewed as a gift and with love. It is a time to sit back and receive as much love as humanly possible by those around you, and most importantly, from yourself.

Sickness is a very important time for love. It's a call for love. Our own love!

Our love, directed inward and straight into the one who has never needed it more, you.

And that is what I love about sickness.

It gifts you literally with LOVE and the opportunity to receive it.

Practice:

The next time you are unwell I want you to do nothing but give yourself love. And receive it from others.

No wallowing in self-pity or focusing on how horrible you feel or unfair it is. Nope, none of that. Your sickness is a gift! Just for you!

An opportunity to do nothing but bask in the love of others, and more importantly, lavish it upon yourself.

The Dining Chairs

Sometimes there are situations or moments in life where there is no possible way you can see love. Situations where your only emotions are the not so pleasant ones, like anger, sadness, disappointment, worry, or even fear. Never love.

This story isn't about any of those emotional feelings, it's about a time when instead of feeling the not so nice feelings, I chose to see love instead. And I saw it in something as simple and every day as old worn dining chairs. Let me tell you more…

It was a typical morning, and I was tidying up when I walked past our almost brand new dining table and its cream white leather chairs.. And again like every other time I passed them, I began to be feel angry and sad and even embarrassment by how damaged the chairs now were. We had barely had them a year!

I could feel the sadness start to take over and it had a grip on my mind and also on me. My mind was now so super focused on every item in our home which was either damaged, broken, second hand or in need of replacing. And I felt crap.

I felt depressed. I felt anything but love.

But then, almost as fast as I started to feel all these things, gratitude stepped in. And boy, did it change things!

As I wiped down the table and worn chairs, I remembered the previous night. It was a Sunday night, a night we all gather together as a family at this table and enjoy a yummy home-cooked meal and tell jokes. I'm serious. We actually tell jokes. I save and gather jokes all week for this particular occasion!

Anyway, as I was thinking about the previous night and all the good times and fun this table and chairs had hosted, I felt grateful. I no longer saw the chairs as ruined. I saw them as loved. So very loved that in their being loved, they were now well worn and used.

Our home is full of 'used' things.

And that's when I realised although our home may be full of used, second hand, and some broken objects. It was also full of 'loved' things.

We don't have many new, fashionable or 'in style' items in our home, most of it is all very loved. And for the first time I could remember, I was ok with that. And not only was I ok with it - I was grateful!

Love had shifted things.

Because not only was I grateful to have these ruined and used chairs in our home, I wanted them!

I wanted them because I no longer saw them as damaged and ruined chairs, but as love. The chairs were now a reminder to me of all the love ever had in our home.

Practice:

Find an item in your home or something in your life, which you really are not happy with. Maybe it's something that disappoints you, or you are struggling to like or accept.

Like I did in the story above, can you flip this? Can you find something you do love about it, and see the blessing and love in what it is you are struggling with?

The easiest way I find to do this is to switch to gratitude. Looking for everything this thing is bringing to you or has brought you. Focusing on everything you love about it and seeing all the good that is in it. Because I am almost certain there will be something, and you will find it.

Naked

One of the most difficult people we will ever come to love, I believe, is ourselves! For me, it has always been one of the hardest and most challenging ways to see love.

Yes, there will be people in our lives who can be awfully hard to love. And there most certainly will be situations which will have you feeling anything but love.

But loving you yourself?

Man, is that a hard one? But ever so necessary!

And sadly, most of us don't love ourselves at all. We expect others to.

In the past I thought I loved myself. On most days I was kind to myself, would treat myself to the occasional massage, and at times would even say out loud, "I love you Nicole." But then I realised something… I really wasn't loving myself at all. Not completely anyway.

To love yourself completely is to love ALL of you. Even the bits you don't want to love. And if you cannot love them, then at the very least accept them.

This reminds me of one time I did exactly that -, I loved all of me. Even the bits I didn't like. And I did it during a difficult time. A time when you are most vulnerable - when you are naked!

Let me tell you more…

I stood in front of my bathroom mirror, completely naked. Standing there naked, I awaited the onslaught. The voice, the criticism, the disgust, yet it wasn't there. And for the first time in as long as I could remember, there was only silence. No voice. No hate.

Where was it?

For years I had hated my body. Had shamed it, criticized it, and looked at my own reflection disgusted.

First, it was because I thought my body was too fat, as I had spent years overweight as a teenager. When I finally lost the weight and was 'skinny', my body wasn't toned, or my stomach flat enough.

And the most recent body part to cop the onslaught of my body hate and non-love was my breasts. They were way too small and not feminine enough (or so I would tell myself).

But one morning, everything changed. As I stood after my shower, completely naked, staring at my reflection in the mirror, something miraculous happened. I didn't see my body as one full of imperfection and faults. I saw love. I saw my body for what it truly was to me, a gift.

I saw my breasts not as too small nor perky or round enough, but as two amazing breasts that had nourished three beautiful boys with milk! And breasts that had never once failed me only ever served and loved me.

And I didn't see a body that was not toned now sagging in parts. I wish it wasn't. But instead I admired how incredibly soft and smooth my skin was. With not one scar or mark on it!

I saw my body at its current weight, although not what I wanted it to be, yet still perfect just as it was.

The biggest revelation and moment came when I looked at my body in all its raw nakedness. And I saw how despite the years of abuse, criticism, over eating, under eating, little exercise, too much exercise, and hate like no other. All my body ever did was love me in return.

My body had never once failed to serve me, or function as she was designed to.

And seeing this I felt so much love for my body that all I could do was pour love, appreciation, and gratitude back into every ounce of my once hated body.

It was amazing. Truly honestly amazing!

There I was, standing looking at myself, not criticising, not critiquing as I usually would, but praising it and feeling an overwhelming sense of gratitude and love for my body. It was unlike anything I had ever experienced. And it was life changing for me, so I decided there and then, this was something I was going to do more often - LOVE my body!

To see my body as beautiful and something which was only ever created for and by love. And choosing to remind myself just how beautiful and perfect my body is, every time a nasty, unkind, or critical thought entered my mind.

No one is perfect. Everyone has something they wish they could change. But do you want to know what I believe is damn sexy?

A person who loves their body regardless!

A person who walks life with love!

Love for themselves, love for others, love for their flaws, and love for the incredible body, which has carried and served them their entire lives.

That is what is beautiful.

For so many years, I didn't walk this walk. Didn't even know or think it was possible. I walked love, don't get me wrong. But the whole time I was walking with love, I hated myself. Hated my body. Hated the way I looked and hated the way my body was compared to others. That isn't love.

Love is acceptance.

Love is gratitude and thanks for everything your body has ever done to serve and love you and loving it back. That is love.

And on the day I stood in front of my mirror completely naked loving myself, I finally got it. Understood love is loving me right now, right here, for who I am.

And my wish for all of you is you too 'get it'. Get that you are enough, get that you are worthy of love right now exactly as you are. And get that whatever you believe you need to be in order to love yourself.

You can love yourself right now, right here, exactly as you are.

What are you waiting for?
Your body loves you. Love it back!

Practice:

Today I want you to love your body. Yep. Your body!

And especially the parts you find hardest to love.

Those parts for whatever reason you dislike most about yourself, I want you to take a moment to love them today.

You can do this by saying out loud, "I love you my thighs, thank you for supporting me and allowing me to bend and sit with such ease."

Or, "I love you wrinkles/grey hair. Thank you for reminding me how far we have come together in life."

Or maybe it is, "I love my body and my weight. As I desire to be healthy, I want to thank you for always being there, to remind me how healthy or even in some cases, unhealthy I am."

Whatever negative, nasty or unloving thought you catch yourself having today about your body, dismiss it, and send this body part love.

I cannot begin to tell you how transformational this practice will be for you. And in time (even in as little as one week), you will see changes within yourself, your own love, and your confidence.

Releasing the Anger

One of the most challenging times to see and express love is when you feel its complete polar opposite – anger!

When you are angry, love has clearly left the building. But … it can return. And the following story is about a time when, although wrapped up in all sorts of anger and feelings, I called on love merely by remembering it and wanting it.

I had been holding on to some serious resentment and anger for almost a week, and it was time to let it go. But I was struggling. Big time.

The anger and resentment was towards my partner Luke, and it was driving me absolutely crazy. I wasn't talking to him and in return, he wasn't talking to me, it had to stop!

It's never any fun when I'm like this. Luke was fine, still going about his life anger and resentment free, but I was not. I was the one in pain and hurting, all because I wouldn't let it go and forgive!

It all started over some damn garlic bread. Garlic bread of all things! So trivial! But isn't it always?

It was around 6 pm on a Saturday, and I had just walked in the door after a full day at work when I noticed garlic bread was still cooking in the oven and everyone was eating dinner.

I asked Luke if he was aware the garlic bread was still in the oven, thinking he had perhaps forgotten about it. And that's when it all started.

Luke suddenly became really defensive and angry towards me. He was being completely unreasonable in his reaction to my simple question and was a total jerk and super mean.

So I called him on his behavior, to which he replied,
"You always walk in the door nagging and complaining."
What?
All I did was ask if he had forgotten about the garlic bread.
So I left him alone for the rest of the evening choosing to keep the peace by saying nothing at all, and walking away.

Yet I took it much further than I had planned as not only did I not say another word to him that night, but kept the silent treatment for days. Days!

I felt horrible, and I wanted it to stop, yet I was still so damn peeved at him. His actions hurt me, and I wanted him to apologise. I knew he wasn't going to because it was clear he had forgotten all about it and was ok.

He (unlike myself) had moved on and was enjoying his days. While I was still holding on to it all, replaying it over and over. And I was becoming angrier by the minute. It sucked!

I had to fix this.

I had to end feeling this way.

And I realised the only way to do it was if I let it all go, FORGIVE him, and look for love.

So I did!

It was damn had. But I did it - I forgave him.

But before I could even get to the step of forgiveness, I had to first see love. I knew deep down Luke didn't want to hurt me that day - I knew he loved me. So I started there, remembering he does in fact love me. And I remembered how much I loved him.

I then thought back to times when I had treated him very similarly to how he had treated me. And I realised whenever I snap, attack, or am horrible to him it is usually because I was already angry, and he had only 'triggered' it!

So with this knowledge I investigated a little further, and you know what I discovered?

I discovered something had happened earlier that day which had caused him to be so angry!

I discovered our boys had broken an expensive electronic device only a few minutes before I had arrived home. Luke was angry about this and had held it all 'in', not wanting to take his anger out on the boys.

Then I arrived home, walked in the door, and questioned some garlic bread in the oven and it was on. All that pent up anger had an opportunity to release.

It's still no excuse to treat someone the way he did me that day, but it happens. I've seen it in me when I lash out at the kids or overreact to something completely insignificant. And because I've seen it before, I was able to see it in him and forgive him.

And once I released all the unforgiveness, anger, and pent up feelings I had against Luke I able to then make room for love to enter. And it did.

It didn't enter with lovey-dovey mushy feelings towards Luke, but it entered with compassion for him, and the really hard day he must have had with the kids when I was at work.

People will, at times, hurt us. And more often than not, it will be unintentional. We cannot escape it. But we can forgive them. It is forgiveness, not for them but also for us. To free us back open to love again.

Practice:

Are you holding onto unforgiveness, or resentment in your heart today?

It's time to let it go and today's practice asks you to do that.

Now I know how difficult this is to do. And I know it's probably the very last thing you want to do right now. But remember, you aren't doing this for other people, but for you.

In fact you don't even need to speak to the person you wish to forgive or let them know you have forgiven them (though if you can please do).

You can do this right here and right now, wherever you are, as true forgiveness takes place in your heart.

Forgive them.

Say it over and over, and over some more, until you feel it fully. Look for love, look for compassion, and feel it for the person who did this to you until it all goes. Free yourself.

Love doesn't hold on to anything.

You Can't Plan Life

Sometimes seeing love, and, feeling it won't come until later. Until after the actual situation, event, or non-loving scenario you found yourself in is over.

I have experienced this many times in my own life.

Times when whatever it was I was going through felt as if it was the worst thing ever to happen to me, and no way ever could any good come of it. Then all of a sudden, it does.

Yep those times.

And they happen to us all.

How in these so-called 'unexpected' 'ruining my life' type moments such great blessings and gifts can be found. Gifts I'm only ever able to receive after the situation has passed and I look for them.

Hindsight. A great thing when it comes to love.

And trust.

Trusting even when you may not feel love is with you, and it always was.

My youngest boy is my best buddy in life. He is my happiness when I am sad, my sanity when I'm losing it, and one of the biggest blessings I've ever received in my life. I absolutely love this boy to bits. Yet it wasn't always this way.

I remember the day I discovered I was pregnant with him, I cried for months. I cried at home, in the toilets at work during lunch breaks, as I fell asleep at night. Every time I remembered I was pregnant with him I cried because I did not want another child.

My life at the time felt ruined. This was not part of what I had planned for my future. I had only just returned to work. My two older boys were finally at an age where I could leave the house and have a social life.

My life was back. And I loved living my life this way!

So the day I discovered I was pregnant and the months following were a massive shock to me. I could almost say I was devastated. And I certainly was not seeing the love in this situation at all.

But as the months passed and life inside me grew, I adjusted. Or more so 'accepted' it. Because I realised life will often have plans for us we don't understand. Yet eventually, like with everything, it will all fit into place and into the perfection of your life.

On 20th March 2012, my youngest son Gabe was born. He entered the world and, at the same time, entered my heart. He was all mine.

And what a gift he was!

Not only to the world, but to me. My life changed dramatically from the moment he was born, and changed in a way it never would have, had he not been born.

For example I left a high paying government job of 10 years, and took on careers and jobs I never imagined myself doing. Like bar work and retail!

And I began to write.

When I look at Gabe I am filled with so much love and gratitude for this boy. A boy I never wanted all because he wasn't part of my 'plan'. A boy who has blessed me beyond anything I could ever imagine.

I've since learnt we can't plan life, only go along with it. And how grateful I am I did, because although at the time I thought my life was over, it was really only beginning.

And now, any time I find myself in a situation where it is difficult to love, or I cannot see it, I remember love is there. It always is. It's just not the time to reveal itself yet.

Practice:

Today I want you to look back over your own life for situations or events which have taken you by surprise and may have even seemed devastating and ask yourself,

Are they still?

Or has this event or situation which was not pleasant at the time, now blessed you in some way?

Maybe it changed the course of your life? Taught you a lesson? Or gifted you with strengths and abilities you didn't know you had?

When you look back on and find love in those not so nice situations in your past, it helps you accept the new ones when they enter your life and fall unexpectedly.

Because you now know, although you may not be able to see it yet, love is there waiting to be revealed in its own time.

Litter Bugs

Love when you're mad? Love when you're disappointed? Love when what someone did was so so wrong?

Yep. Possible.

Possible because I've done it. And it's something I have to work at practicing daily.

It is not always easy to choose to see love when it is difficult, but it is possible.

Like this one time I recall in the following story, when I consciously had to move out of a non-loving state and into one of compassion, forgiveness and then love.

I was driving home late one afternoon behind a car full of young men when suddenly I noticed them wind down their windows and begin throwing empty bottles and trash out of the back of their vehicle.

And man did this annoy me!

Couldn't they hold onto their rubbish a little while longer until they got home?

Is it really ok to just chuck your rubbish out of a moving vehicle onto the road for someone else to later pick it up?

Then I remembered…. I used to do that.

Many, many years ago!

And that's when I forgave them.

Because although there is no way in this lifetime now would I ever do such a thing, I remembered there was once a time in my life when

I did. I was young, self-absorbed, and around the same age these guys were in the car. And I did this same thing.

So how could I continue being angry at them, judging them, and criticizing them when twenty years earlier someone was probably driving behind me, experiencing the same thing I now was?

The roles had reversed.

And, at that moment, I saw it, the love in it all. Without even consciously trying to find the love it just appeared, in the form of compassion and then hope.

I was filled with hope first as I thought perhaps they too would someday realise like I had, how wrong it is to do such a thing. And like me later come to have a complete loathing and almost hatred for such acts.

A change in perspective is everything.

And looking for love in a situation when you aren't feeling it, changes everything!

Love had found me this time, and because it had, I was able to let go of all the anger I felt towards these young men, and not let what I had seen them do ruin my day. And I forgave them like I forgave my younger self many years earlier for doing the same thing.

Love truly can be found in every single situation.

Practice:

Is there something unloving you once did like I had, which you now see others do?

Can you forgive them today and not only forgive them but forgive yourself too?

This doesn't make the act ok, but it does send loving energy into it versus anger, unkindness and hatred! And the world most certainly needs more loving energy. Don't you agree?

And having compassion, love and hope for others will do much for them than hating them ever would.

Love others today. Forgive their 'sinful' actions, and choose to bless them instead.

I Imagine Their Deaths

The ultimate challenge in finding and seeing love in difficult situations would be looking for love in death.

Yet it's possible.

Death, as natural a part of life as it is, can be so devastatingly heart-breaking and painful. And whenever we think about it, find ourselves surrounded by it, or experience it closely when losing someone we love, the last thing we ever think of doing is looking for the 'good' and 'love' in it all.

But death does bring love. And there is love in death.

I wouldn't have known it were possible until I lost my mother at an age far too young. I'll admit, at the time, I didn't see love, only loss. But with time, and even now, as I look back on her death, I see only love.

The following story isn't about death, it is about seeing through it to the love found in it. A love found not only in leaving this world, but also in the very thought of death itself, and allowing it not only to gift you with love, but bless you with it.

A friend of mine once mentioned how this being her last child savored every moment with her. The good times and the bad times! I admit I did this too. And of all the three boys I probably 'savored' – that is, dare I say it, 'enjoyed' Gabe my youngest the most.

I also recall a very odd stage in my life. Whereas, morbid as this is to admit, I would imagine the death of my sons. Every moment I was with one of my sons out of nowhere I'd begin to imagine their passing.

The scenes were graphic and would always result in them dying some terrible death.

It happened so often I was almost afraid to be alone with my boys because sure enough, there it was again, the scene! And all completely unconscious! I had no control over it or when it would occur whatsoever. Honestly, it was horrible, just horrible!

However, what I soon started to notice was although it invoked all sorts of terrible feelings within me, it also left me feeling incredibly grateful for that moment. Grateful for the very moment I had with them right then and now. Alive.

And that is when the love entered this strange morbid stage I went through.

Because every time I would see them dying some horrible death, I would also love them so much more in that moment. So grateful to have them with me alive!

It wouldn't matter their mood, my mood, what they were doing, had done, or how my day had been. Because in that moment, all I saw, felt, and experienced was love!

As crazy as this unconscious habit of mine was it did have some truth behind it.

We are all dying every day.

We don't know when our final day will be. But we do know that someday one day will be our last. And although the chances are very high, my boys will outlive me by many, many years, you still do not know.

Life is never guaranteed.

So this crazy stage I went through in my early parenting years truly did bless me. It had me so much more grateful for every moment I had with my boys. The good times and the bad! Once again proving love can be found in everything, even in your own inner torment it's there, waiting to bless you and waiting to love you.

Practice:

It may sound very strange, but believe me, when you try you will see how incredibly powerful this will turn your heart instantly towards love.

Whenever you find yourself with someone who may be trying your patience, or you feel incredibly frustrated with, or perhaps it's your children who have again gone and done that thing you wish they'd hadn't?

Instead of feeling all the anger, rage, frustration, disappointment, or whatever other not so kind or friendly emotion you currently have going on. I want you to imagine instead the person is dying.

Ok, I hear you. It sounds like a horrible thing to do and plain wrong. And would be, if you wanted them to die.

But you don' t.

You are only 'imagining' they have a few more days of life left.

The reason I'm asking you to do this is because whatever was bothering you so much about the person only moments before will instantly fall away. Most 'issues' with others are so trivial, and although they feel massive at the time, in thelong run, they don't really matter at all.

I have seen so much love and transformations take place on hospital beds. Where all the resentment bitterness, and grudges once held against people, fade away because it 'no longer matters'.

Which is why I question: why wait until someone is dying to forgive them and love them? When you can love them now while they are alive!!

I assure you this is a great little tool to have in your toolbox ready for those hard to love moments and people. Because it works like a charm every time. Enjoy!

Ashamed To Be Fat

Can you see love in pain from your past?

Can you look back upon a time been and gone that was so far from loving that all it caused you was pain and heartache?

Yes!

Because I've done it!

I have looked back on many traumatic times in my own life searching, to find the love in it. And I've found it.

Hindsight is a beautiful thing.

Hindsight can have you seeing love which you did not see at the time., But when reflected upon later, will reveal itself even in the most hard to love situations.

Such a situation for me was my childhood!

And in the following, I share how I reflected back on this time and searched for the love within it. Because I needed to find it!

Needed to know that all the pain, torment, and teenage hell, was somehow worth it, and love was there with me the whole time.

I often take trips down memory lane. In particular, one memory is never a long trip, because it's a memory that has always stayed with me. A memory, which lives in me daily and continues to even to this day.

The memory?

How fat, overweight, chubby - whatever you wish to call it, I once was. And how living this way caused me to feel – not good at all!

I spent most of my childhood and teenage years overweight. It was even something I had kept hidden from my partner Luke for years, as I was too ashamed to tell him. In fact, it was after we had been together for almost ten years (yes, TEN years!) that I told him and showed him a photo of how fat I once was.

Do you know why I did this?

Why I had kept this part of myself hidden from him for almost a decade?

Fear.

And because I was ashamed!

Ashamed by the way I once was and looked. And fearing he, like many, had when I was younger, would tease me, hurt me, leave me and no longer love me because of it.

Silly, I know! But shame does that to you. Childhood wounds and pain do that to you.

However, the day came when I no longer wanted to live this way every time I would think about how fat I once was. With so much pain, shame and disappointment. It was then I knew it was time. Time to search for the gift in it all, time to search for the love. Because as I now know, love is everywhere and would be even in this.

So I looked back, and I began to search for the gift those years had brought me. I admit I had to search long and hard for the love, but guess what? I found it!

Found the gift those torturous years brought me.

Firstly it had led me to where I am to today. A stronger woman. A woman who now knows how much she can survive - how much we all can survive. I suffered from bullying, torment, and a depression so deep I wanted to die. But I didn't.

I survived.

And I thought back to all those people in high school who teased me, hurt me, and bullied me. To the people who had made me fear going to school, and all those who led me to hating myself.

And I thank them.

Because I realised, at that moment, if it hadn't been for all those people who treated me this way, or made me hate myself with as much hate as I did, I never would have been able to learn how to love myself. Or realise how worthy of love I truly am.

They say you have to hit rock bottom before you can ever make your way to the top. Well, that was my rock bottom, and ever since, I have been climbing my way back up.

Climbing back up to where I always belonged, back up to where I should have always been all the time. To a place of worthiness, to a place of deep self-love, and to knowing that no matter how I look, am, or appear to be, I will always be perfectly enough.

And that was how love blessed me in those horrible years of my youth. It blessed me with a gift only later, I would receive…

Knowing who I always was.

And it gifted me with hope.

Because things change, people change and you change. And when in a challenging place and you hit rock bottom, there is only ever one way you can go, up.

I want to add here for anyone who is facing weight problems. It is ok. You are ok. You are not your body any more than you are clothes you wear. You are a beautiful sparkle of love, which shines from within you. A sparkle which will never fade, disappear, or be taken away from you. So let it shine, blinding all those who, for whatever reason, fail to see it.

Practice:

Today's practice is simple. I want you to fully and completely love yourself, no matter what size, shape or weight you are. To love yourself fully and completely no matter how much money you have in the bank, your job title, the clothes you wear or don't wear, and no matter what you own or don't own!

Wherever you find yourself now in life, love yourself fully and completely and as unconditionally as you can. Not just today but every day!

Own Em!

Let me give you an example of a time I saw love. Not at the time, but during its aftermath.

It often happens in the midst of whatever crazy is consuming us at the time. The last thing we ever think of is seeing love!

However, it's often after the storm (or, in my case, fight) has passed, we can then see clearly and look for the love. Because I assure you love will be there, and when you find it, the so-called 'situation' becomes a gift.

Here is an example of such a time for me….

I was not pleasant. In fact, quite horrible. Not my nastiest, because sadly, I've been much worse. But I do remember it wasn't pretty and, well let's be honest, I was acting like a real bitch!

I don't enjoy this aspect of myself either. Still it is a part of me, and as much as I would rather ignore and pretend it doesn't exist, it does.

She nags, throws killer tantrums (those adult ones we all have), is super mean, and no fun to be around at all. I won't go in to details with how I acted this day - you don't need it. I'm sure you can all imagine how I acted, as no doubt you too probably have days and moments like it. Or if you're a male, have been with a woman who has!

Anyway, on this particular day what I loved most was what happened next. How when all the crazy had swept through me, the house, and everything else that was near, I knew almost instantly what I needed to do. Apologise. And to Luke!

It's always him - bless him.

He is always the one to cop the worst of me. He's a strong man, that one. And it must be said we all have that one person in our life who seems to cop the worst of us. The one who tends to bear the brunt of all our not so lovely emotions and anger. And we owe these people in our lives so much more than we give them. We owe them our love.

Which miraculously on this day I did.

Because I chose it.

I apologised to Luke and asked for his forgiveness.

Luke, in his love and goodness, forgave me. And I must add here asking for forgiveness is never easy! Because it means openly admitting we were in the wrong, and in doing so we become vulnerable.

This is why most the time instead of asking for another person's forgiveness we chose to walk off, wait a few hours, days, and in some cases. even years before taking any action. Or we assume everything is forgiven and all is forgotten.

But is it?

I don't think it ever is.

It is why when Luke loved and forgave me it felt so good and only made me want to do the same for him next time it was my turn to forgive him. Because inevitably there'll be a time.

We all have these parts of us which are embarrassing, shameful, and not so lovely, yet is ok. Just own em is all I am saying, and, if you can, apologise and ask forgiveness. Because by doing so, you have found the love in the situation, which was the opportunity to be it.

Practice:

Next time you treat someone poorly instead of just shrugging it off and walking away. I want you personally apologise and ask for their forgiveness.

Now this may be something you already do, and if you do, you are amazing – keep doing it!

But if you are like me (and I suspect most people are), it probably isn't going to be your first reaction to seek forgiveness and apologise, which is why it's today's challenge. And not only for today, but a forever challenge, to make this your new normal. A habit and something you practice daily. Enjoy!

No One Makes It Out Alive

I have an example of seeing love in a time which can be hard to do so. A story I will never forget. And one I love so much I had to share it here.

I love it for many reasons, but mostly because it isn't my own story but of someone I love. Someone who surprised me with seeing love in a situation where I know I would have failed to see any love at all. Never mind finding it funny.

Luke however did both.

Found it funny, and by doing so saw the love.

I share in the hope you can see how in all situations, even those crazy 'why on earth did this happen to me' moments, love still can be found. Even if the only love you find is you laughing at yourself afterwards!

I had had quite the morning, one so bad I decided to call Luke at work and tell him all about it, hoping I'd get a little sympathy. However before I even began to tell him about my morning, he told me about his. And my 'bad' morning all of a sudden seemed pretty insignificant.

Before I even had an opportunity to speak Luke answered the phone and said,

"You're never going to guess what happened to me this morning! It's been eventful."

I didn't try to guess, and even if I had wanted to I never for one moment would have guessed what he said next.

"I was trapped in the work elevator for hours."

He came straight out with it. No lead up, no story detailing how it had happened, just straight up …

"I spent my morning trapped in the elevator at work and they had to send some guys out to rescue me."

You hear about it happening, you see it in movies, but never do you think it actually happens. It does. And to every day normal people like Luke!

What I remember most about this day is how much I loved hearing him tell me this. It completely made my day and took away all the stress, anger and self-pity I felt over my now not so 'bad' morning.

When he told me, I began to laugh like I hadn't in such a long time, it brought so much joy to my soul!

Now, let us get this straight. I wasn't laughing because I wanted Luke to suffer, no, not at all. I'm not that sadistic! I was laughing because as he told me, he too was in hysterics. Laughing like I hadn't heard him laugh for as long as I could remember. We were both in absolute fits of laughter.

And that is all I remember most about this time. The laughter and the joy at Luke being trapped in an elevator for half a day brought us both.

Life isn't serious. It really isn't. Enjoy it. And if you can, laugh at what life sometimes deals you. Luke did.

Luke could have been angry, upset, embarrassed, or allowed what had happened to completely ruin his day. But he didn't. Instead, he chose love by choosing to laugh. And by doing so, it didn't ruin his day, but made both ours!

Practice:

Today I want you to welcome every event, or circumstance that happens to you today with joy!

You missed the bus. Can you laugh about it?

Your children are driving you absolutely crazy! Can you laugh about their crazy antics?

Your date cancelled. Can you laugh about it?

You burnt dinner. Can you laugh about it?

Today's challenge is simply this. To bring more love into your day by bringing in more joy, and choosing to laugh at everything which would normally steal it.

Treasure The Moments

When my youngest son Gabe was a baby, he would often have great difficulty in getting to sleep. It would make me so cranky!

One night, in particular I remember quite clearly, because I almost resented him for it. Until in a split moment, everything changed.

Love entered.

And what only moments earlier, was filling me with frustration, anger, and rage was now filling me with love.

I share this story as an example of how quickly a change of perspective can take you from one so called 'bad' moment, into one of gratitude, love and even reverence.

I hope this story fills you with as much love as does for me to recall it…

It was like most nights when Gabe was this age - no matter how hard I tried, he just would not sleep!

He would climb in and out of his cot, leave his room, re-enter his room, play with some toys, climb back into his cot, and then start the whole routine again! It drove me nuts. But on this one particular occasion when it was now long after midnight and the whole carry on had been going for hours. I was done.

I was beyond tired, had tried everything I knew, and I no longer had any patience for him whatsoever. And whatever little love I had was quickly being eaten up by anger and resentment.

I only had only one option left.

To pull out the one tactic and tool I hadn't used since he was a baby. Which was to pick him up, place him in my arms, and start rocking him to sleep like there was no tomorrow – all 12kgs of him!

As I began to walk him around the room, rocking him in my arms like I once did when he was newborn baby, something miraculous happened. He fell to sleep in my arms. Almost instantly, in fact!

And in that moment all the anger and frustration I had felt, left. Because as I looked down and saw my almost three-year-old sleeping so peacefully in my arms, it made the past few hours worth it.

The getting up, how tired and cranky I was, the frustration, all of it worth it, just for this moment. This very moment right here and now, the one I was now experiencing with Gabe in my arms.

As I watched him lay sleeping in my arms, no longer did I see a toddler who wouldn't sleep anymore, I saw a little boy. A little boy who would soon someday be a man.

I could have rocked him forever that night, knowing the day will soon come when I'll no longer be able to. And how soon he will be a fully grown man living his own life outside of mine. And I'll no longer be able to cradle him in my arms, but it will be his time to cradle his ownbaby in his.

Allow love to enter.

Treasure the moments, all the moments. Because they pass so quickly and when they do you can never go back and return.

Practice:

Moments don't last forever. They pass. Today pick a moment from your day and savor and enjoy it. It could be a phone call from a friend, drinking a cup of tea or out walking your dog.

As you have this 'moment' be aware how in only a few short minutes, hours, or days it will soon be gone forever and no longer a moment but a memory.

Knowing this, knowing it will pass. Does it change your experience? Does it make you appreciate it more and love it more fully?

Only one way to find out. Try it!

And the best bit about this practice is it can be reversed.

It can be used in moments you don't enjoy so much, like going to the dentist, cleaning the house, awkward and uncomfortable moments, or those tasks you've been putting off.

Because all moments pass. The good and the bad. And knowing this has helped me more times than I count.

Part Two
Choosing Love

"Everything in life always starts with a single choice."

Choosing To Love Others

"Love is the bridge between you and everything."

Love can be such a funny thing. And relationships with others I believe, is the brewing ground for it all.

There is always heartache and joy, good times and bad. But love is love. And it's also why I believe we must consciously decide to love others. Because, at times, it will be challenging to do so.

Yet love is a commitment, a commitment you make between you and the person who stands before you. It can be with a friend, stranger, lover, neighbour, or even yourself.

I've never personally spoken this commitment out loud, in a church, or have it documented somewhere official. But I committed to myself to choose love and to practice it daily.

Sometimes I get it right, so right, and I'm on fire with loving others and myself. And other times, well, let's say love has clearly left the building!

But one thing remains the same every single time.

Love is a choice.

A choice we all can make.

And I assure you, as I have seen in my own life after years of practicing this, that when you choose to love, it is always, always, the right choice. Every single time!

Olga

Sometimes choosing to love others can be choosing it when you don't even really know how to. All you do know is you are one hundred percent committed to loving this person and will do whatever it takes to do so.

Sometimes loving them may be as simple as offering a biscuit with their tea, holding their hand, carrying their luggage, or offering to drive them somewhere. The main thing is you chose for one reason only, to love people.

How that looks will always be different.

But one thing remains the same. Love. No matter how love is wrapped, delivered, or given, it will always be love and will always be a choice YOU get to make.

So choose it.

Love is an action. It is never passive.

And the following is an example of how I loved a dear friend of mine simply by doing nothing at all except choosing to love.

I knew a lady. Her name was Olga and she lived in an aged care facility. She didn't speak much, hardly at all, and our conversations were never deep.

But you know what?

It didn't matter.

What matters is I was there.

What matters is I loved her. And I chose to do so.

I would hold her hand, listen when she spoke, wipe the food from her chin and offer her tissues when she wept. I never thought I did much, wondering some days if me even being there mattered because there was more I could or should be doing to help!

But then I realised something not long after she passed away. I did do something every single time I visited her. I loved her.

Every visit, the love would look different, but it was always love, and it was still a choice I had to make. Because just by showing up each day, I was choosing love, and I was choosing her.

So many senior people live every day so alone. They live in their own fancy homes, or not so fancy, some in newly built modern establishments, like Olga's. Many of them have access to the latest technology, TVs, healthcare, and three delicious meals a day.

But you know what?

None of it means anything to them.

And it never will or could ever replace what you and I can give them. Love. Because love isn't in things, it's in you! It's in me; it's in us all!

All they want, all they seek, and all they crave is for someone to love them. For someone to care about and show up, reminding them they matter and mean something to someone.

People would often tell me what I did for Olga during the last stages of her life was so kind and so great. It wasn't.

I did nothing special at all.

I just showed up each day and loved her. I loved her by being there and doing so, reminded her someone loved her.

It doesn't take much to love someone. But it will always require a choice. And most of the time that choice is you choose it. Choosing to love the people in whatever way you can, however that may look.

Practice:

Is there someone in your life you want to love but are not sure how to do this?

Could you already be loving them without even realising it by simply being you? By being there?

Or maybe you've wanted to love in a way you thought was too small or insignificant so you didn't?

I challenge you today to love someone simply by being you. Doing nothing special at all except offering all of who you are to them, in whatever way they need it.

"You Are Such A Good Driver."

I remember one time I consciously chose to love. I remember it so clearly because it was precisely that, a decision! A decision I had to make because I was about to choose anything and everything but love!

I also remember it so vividly because of its amazing and instant result.

When tempted to judge and criticize this person - which sadly is often a favorable and almost automatic choice of mine, I didn't. And instead consciously decided to love the person instead. This is how it all went...

We were on our way out together as a family to have some fun. Luke my amazing man was driving. He always does, and I love he does. But something I don't love so much he drives so freakin damn slow, and I'm always in a hurry to be somewhere!

So there we all were. Luke, driving the speed limit - which to me at the time felt soooo slow. And there I was in the passenger seat, all seething and ready to lay it all out and criticize him. I could feel it all bubbling up - I was ready to explode and say something.

But then this thing happened.

My total perspective changed!

It turned around completely. All because I heard a voice say, "Praise him Nicole. Bring him up not down. Choose love.

"Tell him how great he is. Look for the good in this - it's there."

So I did. I chose it, chose love.

I chose to bring him up not down, and commend him not condemn him. And you should have seen his face.

Total shock.

Yet, at the same time, real pride. If Luke weren't a man, I'd almost say he was glowing.

All because, instead of coming out with some snide remarks at the speed that we were traveling, I didn't. And instead, I chose love and said …

"You are such a good driver. You really are. I've never taken the time to tell you just how much I admire you for never having had any accidents or even one single speeding ticket, unlike myself. We both know I've had a few. You're awesome at driving."

And it was the truth.

I had taken the focus off my own inner frustration at being late and him driving 'slow' (which in actual fact was the speed limit). And had turned the whole situation around by finding the love and sharing it! And all in milliseconds!

He was surprised, and I too was surprised I had actually said it. I think it shocked us both. Yet when I looked over at Luke I could see it, there on his face, a little smirk, he felt proud. He felt good. He felt appreciated and he felt loved!

Because let's be honest - what man doesn't want to be complimented on their driving?

What I loved most about this day was what I learned. I learned how something as simple as a change in attitude changes everything. The mood in the car, of me, of Luke, and the mood for the rest of the entire day!

He is a great driver. Cautious and a little slow at times, yes. But unbelievably good and precise.

Me?

I'm always in a damn hurry and expect everyone else to be!

And that, my friend, is wrong. Wrong because it may be the way I do things, but that doesn't mean it should be everyone else's way too.

Great lesson I learnt that day.

The lesson of praising and bringing others up, not down. And the lesson of how quickly a mood can change when you simply change your own damn attitude and choose love.

Practice:

Yep you guessed it!

Today's practice is to lift someone up not bring them down.

Is there a little 'quirk' about someone you know or love that tends to rub you the wrong way? Or maybe there is something you are having a hard time loving?

It could be someone never putting items back where they go or leaving cupboard doors open. Maybe it's the way they chew their food or snore in their sleep?

Ok now flip it.

Can you praise them on it?

Can you find something about it that you do love? And when you do, can you now love them for it and even so much as praise them for it?

It may be a challenge, but it's possible. Try it today, and be sure to let me know how you go!

Lady In The Waiting Room

There are millions of people suffering in the world, and often it can seem so overwhelming, as though there is nothing we can do. And anything we did do would be so insignificant it would barely make a difference.

I struggled with this for many years. It seemed so hopeless.

Surely I can do something!

Surely making a choice to choose love every day will make a damn difference?

And my friends it does.

Because although you cannot love every person on this planet or help the many millions in need.

You can help one.

The one who stands in front of you at this moment. Help them. One person. It matters.

And in the following I share about a time by choosing to love 'just one' I helped this 'one' suffer a little less.

As life will so often have it, it will test you. On your word. On your truth. On your integrity and on all you believe and say.

It's as though God says,

"Let's see how serious you are about this."

He did this exact thing for me not so long ago.

Shortly after sharing a video and expressing to friends how we cannot save the world and love everyone, we can still love one person and the little patch of earth we are in. Before long God or, as you may prefer to call it 'life', tested me.

I was sitting in the doctor's waiting room with my youngest son when it happened. I noticed a woman. It was hard not to notice her. Everyone in the room had her. Not only by the way she smelt but by the abuse and attitude she was now hurling towards the place.

And that's when God spoke and I heard it. The voice.

"Will you love someone for me, Nicole?"

"Will you sit with this woman in her pain, one who is hurting?"

Nope. No thanks. I don't want to was my initial response. But it was too late. The woman had now made eye contact with me and was trying to bring me into the debate she was having with the staff.

I kept up the eye contact and listened to her, looking for a way out.

Thankfully I remembered my very own words.

Words I had only spoken and shared with others a few days earlier. How so many are suffering in this world and although we may not be able to save them all, we certainly must not add to it!

So there I was looking at this woman, a toxic negative person and someone in society I would do everything in my power to avoid.

But I didn't. Not this time because I remembered.

Remembered love.

Remembered why I'm here. Why you're here. Why we are all here.

And I chose it. Chose love.

I got up from my seat and went and sat next to her. I put my arm around her and sat with her as she verbally abused life, complained, and expressed everything in her heart that she needed to express.

Some of it quite malicious.

Then something miraculous happened.

The words. The hate. All that venom turned into tears and she wept in my arms.

And only then could I love her. In fact I already had.

By listening.

By allowing her the space to express her pain without me adding to it. And as she spoke and complained about the doctors, the wait time, and all her aches and pains. I didn't add to it. Didn't agree with her or confirm everything she was saying.

No.

I simply just listened.

And after a few minutes she came to her own realisation and said,

"I'm sorry. I'm in so much pain. I'm so tired. My son died a few years ago and I haven't been the same since. I'm not coping. I know I'm overreacting, and it isn't the doctor's fault I've been sitting here for 40mins, but it's all just too much for me right now."

And the tears fell some more, and the healing began.

But to get to this point of healing, she needed to get it all out. And me sitting there next to her, holding her, listening to her speak without judgement or adding more fuel to the fire, she was able to get it all out and feel what needed to to be felt.

It took courage on my part. But mostly, it took my time and for me to put my own selfish needs aside for a few minutes.

There is so much suffering in this world. More than any of us alone could ever stop.

But we can help one person.

We can help someone suffer a little less in their pain by simply being there.

Love doesn't ignore pain. It sits with it and holds its hand until it passes.

And that is exactly what I did with the lady in the waiting room.

Practice:

Next time you see someone in pain and perhaps expressing it in a not so nice way, don't walk away, ignore them or leave them - love them.

This could be something as simple as looking over at them making eye contact. Or giving them an assuring look or smile that simply says, 'its going to be ok.'

It could be listening to someone like I had as they rant and rage, not offering advice, making them right or wrong, just listening.

Or it could be offering someone a tissue, asking if they are ok and holding their hand.

I cannot say how it will look or what you are to do. Only you will know what is right in that moment. The one thing I can say for sure is loving people is not ignoring them or walking away. It's being there in whatever way you can.

Admit You're Wrong

Love is always a choice. And loving others is a choice all of us must make every day if we want to live peaceful, happy, and loving lives. This is why one day, I chose it. Not at the time, I admit, but afterward.

But that doesn't matter.

It never matters when you choose it, or how long it takes you to choose it, only that you do. And that day, I chose love by admitting I was wrong.

I had said some things during a phone call with someone I love, which I later regretted. I was not supportive or loving towards them when usually I would be. Instead, I had spoken to them with anger and frustration, inflicting all of my own issues, opinions, and thoughts onto them.

And not in a nice way either!

But in one of those completely uninvited, unwarranted, demeaning, and demanding kind of ways. Afterwards, I felt terrible. And I know this is because I wished I'd handled it differently. I wished I had chosen love.

The old 'pre choosing love' me would have sat with these feelings for days. I was feeling all those terrible emotions such as guilt, remorse, and regret. And even perhaps a little later convincing myself how the person might have deserved the way I had spoken to them, and how right I was for doing so.

In fact I may have even been right this time, but it did not matter or change the way I felt in the moment. And because I hadn't treated this person with the respect and love we all deserve, I knew what I needed to do, fix it and fast.

I knew if I wanted to rid myself of the horrible feelings I was now feeling and restore the relationship, I had to choose love.

So how did I choose it?

As I wasn't in the space or ready to speak with them yet, but I emailed them (and let's be honest, sometimes an email is a heck of a lot easier).

In the email I apologised for the way I had spoken and asked if they could forgive me. They did, and not only did they forgive me, but asked if I could forgive them also.

And you know what I learnt in all this?

How opening ourselves up to others, admitting when we are wrong, and choosing love, only ever leads to better relationships and happier feelings.

It's hard to admit when we are wrong, especially when we have stepped out of line. But what good does it do if we don't do this? The relationship is always the one that suffers.

And I am grateful for that one weekend where I discovered personal relationships are far more important than my own pride and being right.

Practice:

Is there someone today you can apologise to?

Have you said something recently that you have later regretted?

Or is there a relationship in your life that needs a little bit of a love boost?

Today I challenge you to restore the relationship by humbling yourself and rebooting some love back in by apologizing for past events, admitting your part in it, and asking for forgiveness.

If you are unable to do this in person, you could message them or send a card. It doesn't matter how you do it, only that you do. And do it with the full sincerity and intention of your heart.

The Telemarketer

I love how love is a choice, and how it's always in our power to choose it. At any given moment, we can either choose to love, or choose not to love. The choice is always ours.

And the power (oh how I love power) is also ours to use. We are the only ones who decide whether we want to be loving and kind. No one can make us do it, only we can.

It's what I love most about living life this way.

Living a life where you consciously choose to love others. And in the following story, I share about a time I deliberately chose to love a telemarketer. The very type of person who can trigger in me many non-loving feelings and actions. But not this day. Because this day, I claimed the power. The power to choose! And I decided love.

I was already irritable, I was moody, and I was not having a good day. And then the phone rang. On the other end was some lady trying to sell me something. I wasn't in the mood for this at all. Nor the slight bit interested in whatever she had to sell.

But then there it was. The inner voice I often hear, the voice reminding me to choose love.

"Love her Nicole. Love her."

I wondered how I could do this?

How could I love some stranger on the other end of the phone who I didn't even know? And how could I love her when I was already in such a bad mood myself?

Then I realised I could, and it was easy. Simple in fact!

I could be kind, I could be courteous, and I could allow her to speak and listen to all she had to say even if I wasn't going to commit to anything or buy anything from her. I could listen and then kindly say no.

The very least I could do was offer her the simple courtesy of letting her finish before cutting her off or hanging up. I could even bless her with compliments and be sympathetic to all she had probably been put through by other callers before me.

So this is exactly what I chose to do. And I did it.

At the end of our phone call she said,

"Wow. I wish everyone were as nice and kind and as you. Most people just hang up on me or are rude."

Sadly I am usually that person.

And even seconds before answering the phone this time I was tempted to be one of those people again and hang up on her. But I didn't and hopefully never will be again.

Telemarketers are people too, people just like you and me. They are working to pay bills and support themselves and their family. They deserve our respect, kindness, and our love. Let's choose it.

Practice:

Next time a telemarketer calls you, or you see someone selling something in a store, be kind, be nice, stop and say hello. Give them your time, give them a smile. Listen to them.

But mostly, just love them.

You don't have to buy anything. I promise. And if they get a little too 'pushy' on you, you can wish them a great day and walk away, or simply end the call and hang up.

Messy Rooms

Choosing to love others can often be letting go of what bothers you most about them. To overlook those little nuisances and behaviors they possess, which quite frankly tick you off!

Because love doesn't blame, love doesn't nag, nor does love criticise or condemn. It only ever loves.

And the following is about a time when love was completely present in the building because I did not nag, criticize, condemn, or even complain, as tempting as this was to do!

Instead I accepted what was before me, chose love, and in return received gratitude.

Let me share with you all how.

Walking into my eldest son Hugh's room I saw every single item of clothing he had ever owned scattered all over the floor. In fact the floor was no longer visible. He was at school, and wouldn't be home for hours, and I had a choice. I could bend over and pick up every item of clothing on the floor or leave it.

No way could I leave this mess, it would drive me crazy all day! So I bent over and started picking up all the clothes. And as I did, I decided not to let it bother me and to forgive my son. To let it go, accept that he is a 'messy kid' compared to his brothers, and choose love.

I looked at the clothes scattered all over the floor and thought to myself, "Wow he has so much. How great is this!"

And, I had done it. I had chosen love.

Because when I looked down again at the pile of clothes, I realised how blessed we must be to be able to buy our son so many clothes.

I looked one last time at the mountain of clothes on the floor and realised something else. It can mean only one thing - a boy to fill all these clothes.

A Child!

Children to love!

Children to pick up after!

I have children!

I had been blessed with children when not all of us are. And I had chosen love and chosen to love my son. To overlook the mess and to ignore this age and stage he was going through.

And it changed everything,

Because love does that, it changes you.

It changes your mood, your day, and will your life. And the very best thing of all - it always leaves you feeling fantastic. This is exactly the reason I make the conscious decision each day to choose love.

I encourage you to try it, to choose love daily. And even if you do not do it as often as you would hope or would like, I promise you when you do it, it will be powerful. And over time, it will not only transform your days but your life. Like it has mine.

Practice:

Today's challenge is to choose love *consciously* every moment you remember.

You're washing the dishes. Can you choose love here?

You're picking your kids up from school. Can you choose love here?

You have a work meeting today your dreading. Can you choose love here?

It's late at night, the day almost over. Can you choose love right now in this moment?

The variety of ways in which you do this is endless. It could be running you or a loved one a bath if it is late. It could be treating your kids to an afternoon play at the park or icecream after school.

It could be listening to your co-workers (I mean really listening) and encouraging them as you do. Or maybe it is something small like offering to clear the water glasses and tucking in all the chairs?

So many ways every day we can all choose love and do it. And today, I am challenging you to do it and do it as many as you can in the next 24 hours.

It Transforms You

Choosing love is often (if not most of the time) choosing to change your perspective. And with a change of perspective comes a change of heart. And this change of heart is often all that is needed to get us right back into loving others.

The quickest way to do this I have found is with gratitude, where instead of focusing on all which is going wrong in our lives and the non-loving moments, we look for loving ones.

In the following I share an example from my own life where I had to use a little change of perspective and gratitude to move out of what I was feeling and right back into love.

And of all things to take me out of love, you would never have guessed it was a damn garbage bin to do so!

It always amazes me how we are as humans and the things we allow to strip us from loving others.

I was changing the kitchen bin for the third time this week, except this time I had hit my limit because as I was changing the bin I began to notice myself becoming really angry. I was cursing, abusing, blaming, and firing some serious venom towards Luke.

All this was happening inside my head of course, and was only being made worse by me adding to it with thoughts such as …

"Why am I the only one who ever does this?"

"Isn't it a man's job to empty the bins?" And then attacking him some more with,

"When was the last time he did it anyway? I'm forever doing it."

I was becoming madder with every new thought I had. And I certainly wasn't feeling any love towards him whatsoever. How could I?

It was his fault!

He should be emptying the bins not me! He had caused all this anger.

But then another voice entered my head, the voice of gratitude, the voice of love. The one which reminds me to love others and it said,

"You are emptying bins Nicole, calm down."

"Look how blessed you are!"

"Look how good you have it where to empty garbage and remove rubbish from your home all you need to do is take it outside a few meters, then in a few days a big truck comes along and takes it all away for you."

I much preferred this voice.

Because it was right.

My life is simple and blessed!

Rubbish, which let's admit, is no fun and not something many of us want to be dealing with! Is cleared away and removed from our homes weekly. And we need not do a thing except empty our bin, replace the bag, and carry it outside to a bigger bin where a garbage truck will come along and take it away.

And there I was complaining about it.

And where was Luke anyway while I was doing all this?

At work!

Earning money to provide for us as a family, so I can stay at home and enjoy our children (and empty garbage bins).

Gratitude will change your life - if you let it.

And a change of perspective is the quickest way to move you into gratitude every single time.

That day with the bins I was on a quick downhill spiral towards everything love is not! I was angry, resentful, and in the worst mood ever, all because I was changing a bin. All because I had made up some story about how 'unfair' it all was.

Love doesn't do this.

Love doesn't make you or others wrong; it gets the job done. And gets it down with joy, gratitude, peace, and every other feel-good emotion.

This is why we must choose to love the moment we feel ourselves slipping.

And one of the quickest ways I know how is by changing your perspective and switching over to gratitude. Because once you do, I assure you love enters every single time.

Practice:

Is there something that you find really hard to be grateful for?
Something, which seems like a curse rather than a blessing?
Can you switch this around?
Change your perspective a little?
Let some gratitude in? And then see the love in it all?
Because if what I believe is to be true, then love will be there.
It has to be!
You only need to look for love by choosing it. So today's practice is to look for an area or place in your life where you currently struggle to see love, and look for it by changing your thoughts about it and perspective.

I Stopped

Loving others doesn't necessarily always require much action on your part. It can be something as simple as listening, stopping, or giving another person your time.

Even words aren't always needed to love others. In fact words play only a small part in our love. Because love as we know, is an action, an action which can be something as simple as being there or stopping and taking the time to listen.

The following is about a time I did both.

I was in a large shopping centre with my youngest son Gabe to meet a friend for coffee. Walking to the coffee shop to meet my friend we passed an elderly lady pushing a large shopping cart full of her purchases.

The elderly lady stopped as she passed us, looked down at my son Gabe, then back up at me and said, "What a cutie."

He is. And he was especially cute at this age, as he was going through that adorable stage all toddlers go through.

Usually when this happened (and surprisingly it happened often), I would say, 'Thank you' or 'Yes he is', smile, and keep walking. I would never stop. But this time was different.

Because I chose love.

And I decided to stop.

We exchanged small talk about his age, the day, the weather, but then out of nowhere, she began to tell me all about her sons who had now grown up to be doctors. She told me all about their wives, their lives, and their children – her grandchildren.

And you should have seen the joy in her eyes as she spoke of them all. I hardly said a word. I didn't need to. She was in so much delight at being able to share her joy and love of her family with someone who would listen.

Me.

All because I stopped and took the time to listen.

It was ten minutes of my life, ten minutes I'll never get back.

But you know what?

I wouldn't want it back. Because those ten minutes had gifted this lady with love.

I had heard her. I had listened, and I had given her the opportunity to relive and share the joy in her life. All because I stopped, put my own needs and to-do list aside for 10 minutes, and love someone.

Everyone has a story, but not everyone hears it. Next time someone wants to share theirs, listen. Because it is one of the most beautiful ways, you can love them.

Practice:

Next time you ask someone how their day was or someone stops to talk to you about the weather or whatever it is. Stop. And take the time to listen. The challenge is not to say much at all, but rather listen and see what they have to say.

Listening is one of the most significant ways we can love people. Many people in the world want to be heard, but no one ever wants to listen, only talk. Today I challenge you (and for the entire week!) to talk less and listen more. Because I assure you so many gifts and treasures await in others stories.

The Icing Sugar

Loving others will often require a little sacrifice on your part. I know you all don't want to hear this, but it's true. And it will at times requir a little bit of you, and probably a whole lot more of your time.

Time, being so precious and limited these days, is such a beautiful gift to give. So when you do give of your time, it is always that extra little bit special.

The following is about a time I chose love by deciding to sacrifice a little of my own time.

'Yay', I thought to myself, 'Almost finished.' I was in the last aisle of the grocery store picking up the final items I needed when an older man from behind me called out.

"Excuse me," he said pulling out an old tattered shopping list from his back pocket.

"Can you help me"?

"Sure," I said secretly delighting in it as I love helping others, especially the elderly.

"Do you know what icing sugar mixture is and where I can find it? I've been up and down every aisle and I can't seem to find it anywhere," he said flustered.

"My wife gave me this list." He continued.

"Look, it says it right here - icing sugar mixture," he told me as he pointed to and pronounced each word separately, which was hand written on his shopping list.

I smiled. Noticing the other items listed on the piece of paper, his wife must be baking a cake, I thought to myself.

I told him I knew what icing sugar mixture was and where to find it. Then I explained it was kept over in the cake and sugar aisle and pointed in its direction.

He had no clue what I was talking about or where the cake and sugar aisle was. I would say he looked even more confused now with all my pointing and directing than he had before he approached me.

This is when I noticed something about myself I didn't know up until now, and I want to share it with you all.

I didn't want to help him anymore.

Why?

Because it was too hard, taking too much of my time, and quite frankly, the bloke didn't seem to understand me at all. And this so-called pleasant 'loving' situation which I thought it would be, had quickly turned into something entirely different - an annoying situation that was getting me all frustrated and angry.

But because I am committed to practicing this love thing and because the 'voice' of love is now so active in my life, I heard it say "Nicole, go with him. Take him to the aisle."

But I still did not want to.

I had my youngest son Gabe with me, and I was almost finished with my shop and was about to leave. And the darn icing bloody mixture was six aisles down!

So I start thinking.

How do I get out of this?

How can I help him without offering to get it for him?

This lasted barely a minute because the 'voice' came back.

"Nicole. Help this man. It isn't about you. It is about him. So it will mean walking a few aisles out your way and returning but so what!

You're able-bodied and this man is elderly and clearly needs your help. And some day you'll be elderly just like him and may need the help."

The voice was right. So I said to the man,

"Here. Follow me. I'll take you to the icing sugar." And I did, with my full trolley and my youngest son Gabe tagging along all the way back to aisle seven.

Love.

It knows.

Love always knows what's right, when it's right, and how to do it. The only problem is us, our plans, our precious 'time', and whatever other blocks we put up between love and loving others.

I am still to this day grateful for this man and his icing sugar mixture because I will never forget it. Never forget how quickly and easy it was for me to almost turn down an opportunity to love someone, all because I didn't want to help or have the time.

Practice:

Next time you catch yourself saying no or blocking an opportunity to love someone all because you don't have the time or don't want to, don't. See if you instead can push past all that and love them. Because I assure you this is most certainly the more loving and higher road to travel.

Do I Ignore Or Say Hi?

I say it often but only because it's true.

Love is always a choice.

You have to CHOOSE love, even when it may not necessarily be what you want to do at that moment. Even when it may make you feel uncomfortable, awkward, or seem a little embarrassing!.

Because the truth is most of the time, none of these things ever eventuate, and even if they did, your loving action will always be worth it and override any discomfort.

Whenever you choose to love someone despite how you feel or despite the response it may produce, you choose to let love rule your life and not fear.

The following is an example when fear wanted to overrule my choice in loving someone, and I almost let it.

Until I didn't.

I let love win. I let love rule. And by doing so allowed love to overpower my choice.

I was grocery shopping (as I so often am when these love opportunities present themselves) when I happened to notice an older lady who I immediately recognised. She was someone who came into my workplace regularly.

I contemplated whether to approach her and say hi or ignore her and pretend I hadn't seen her. My lack of self-confidence at the time and fear of feeling awkward had me choose the latter. And I convinced myself if she were to make eye contact with me, or I bump into her, only then would I say hi.

Well as life so often has it, I did bump into her. In the cat food aisle!

She was standing directly in front of the cat food I needed and, for me to grab our cat some food, I would need her to move. Perfect opportunity.

I tapped her on the shoulder and said,

"Hello, I cannot remember your name but I recognise you from work." (probably part of the reason I had the fear to approach her to begin with). And I mentioned my place of work.

She didn't recognize me at all.

Awkward!

Yet I don't blame her. I was out of uniform, had a toddler with me, and was not looking my usual made up self like I do when I work. But after a few seconds and a bit of prompting, she knew who I was. We had a short conversation, I grabbed the cat food, and I left.

Afterwards I wondered what the point of all this was.

Why did I see her?

Did I really need to say hi?

Did it achieve anything? Didn't seem like it!

Then I realised it did. I had loved her.

I loved her because what I had done was more than a simple hi and hello. I had recognised her, acknowledged her, and made her feel as though she were more than just another customer to me. She was someone.

Someone I remembered, someone who mattered and someone worthy of stopping for and to wish a blessed and happy day.

Life is simple like that at times. People will be placed on our path only for us to say hi, hello, how are you, have a great day, and goodbye. Whilst others are placed on our paths for a lot more. Only you can determine this.

But one thing is for sure, everyone who is placed on your path is done so for a reason. To be loved by you in whatever way possible. No matter how simple, how small, or how insignificant it may seem.

Practice:

Today when you are out and about, notice everyone who has been placed on your path and see if you can love them in some way. Maybe you will know them, maybe you won't, but don't let this stop you!

Can you say hello? Smile at the stranger passing by? Open a door for someone? Lend a helping hand or ask someone how their day is going?

What the action looks like won't matter, what matters is the love behind it.

Today have the intention to love people placed on your path. Don't worry about how it will look or how you will do it, because trust me, the action will almost always automatically follow.

My Way - The Right Way?

Now, this is a hard one to practice, well, at least for me, it has been the most challenging - to love others by allowing them to be right in what they believe is right, even when you think they are not!

Or how about letting others have their own way when you are convinced your way is so, so, much better?

Love never demands its own way. It doesn't control or boss others around, and it certainly doesn't try to convince it's right and others are wrong.

No, love loves. That's all it does! And it loves by letting others be well, them.

The following is about a time when I thought what I was doing was loving, when it wasn't. It was overpowering and demanding. Perhaps you can relate?

I went through a stage once of giving my boys pikelets for lunch. Do you know those teeny tiny little mini pancakes? They were the perfect size for small hands, super easy, and the best bit, my boys loved them!

Gabe, my youngest, would have jam and cream the only way to have them if you ask me (or anyone else for that matter), but Julian my middle son, well, he wanted vegemite and cream. Vegemite alone would have been strange on a sweet pikelet, but to mix that savoury, salty Australian black spread with cream, well, um, no.

I started to tell him why he couldn't have vegemite and cream and how it was a silly idea and would taste disgusting. I even tried to convince him to have Jam and cream like his brother and told him how much nicer it would taste.

But when I looked at my seven-year-olds face and saw how excited and happy he was to have a pikelet with vegemite and cream and then his face immediately drop the moment I told him he couldn't, I stopped myself. Because it was only then I realised something...

How often I actually did this.

How often I would insist 'my way' was the right way. That I knew best.

Which is true. I do know what's best. But only what's best for ME, not others!

By me denying Julian his choice of spread just because I thought it was the worst combination ever, I realised it was not love.

Love would never demand others eat only what you like, and when they do choose something you don't enjoy, go on to convince them how wrong they are in their choice! No. That is not love. Love allows others freedom and their choice.

Personally, I couldn't think of anything worse on a pikelet than vegemite and cream, but for Julian, perhaps it was the best combo ever. So I made it – vegemite and cream, on a pikelet, and he ate the whole thing. He even asked for seconds!

Afterwards, I wondered what would have happened if I hadn't chosen love and made Julian eat what I wanted?

What would this tell him?

On a deeper level it would tell him he doesn't know what's best for him and how he should always do what others insist - not what he himself knows to do.

Not a message I want to be teaching my boys.

And, certainly not a way to love others.

Yes, there will be many times when we know what is best for our children and our way will be right. As we always will be and are the parent.

But many of those times, I now question and discern. Because often (like the time with the pikelets), it may not be a matter of me knowing what's best, but thinking I do.

If I can make any suggestion at all, it would be to follow your heart and let love choose, because love gets it right every single time.

Practice:

Is there an area in your life where you believe you know best and your way is right?

Or has someone ever suggested something that you think is completely outrageous or you know for a fact is wrong?

Ok, so this is where your challenge comes in. Not to say anything. At all. And to love anyway, letting them be and keeping any suggestions or opposing opinions to yourself.

Give it ago, you will find this act of love is much harder to do than it seems.

Wet Pants

Choosing to love others is choosing to forgive. And forgiveness is probably one of the most challenging ways ever to love someone. Because often forgiving seems like we are letting them off the hook.

But forgiveness isn't that at all.

It's choosing love.

I have many examples in my own life of when I have had to forgive others. And the one I am going to share here is very basic. And although it may be a basic type of forgiveness it was not necessarily easy to do at the time.

Because when you embark on the life-changing path of choosing to love others, it will more often than not involve forgiveness. And almost (if not every time), involve some serious effort on your part. And on this particular day with my son, it involved a whole lot of strength to keep my cool and not lose it.

My middle son had wet his pants, right there in the middle of the kitchen floor. He wasn't young either, old enough to know better. He had been toilet trained for quite a few years, so this was not at all what I was expecting to find on a Monday morning on the way out the door.

And here it was, another one of those moments. Those moments where your automatic reaction is to yell, get mad, scream at your kids, completely lose it, and choose anything and everything but love.

I could feel it all starting to build up, the anger, the frustration because we would all now be late. And not only was there a massive puddle of wee to clean up in the kitchen but also wet clothes and underwear to find and deal with too!

I remember my son walking into the kitchen and looking at me. It was a look I will never forget. A look of utter fear. And deep, deep remorse.

And I was thankful he did.

Because it was this look, and the moment he looked at me, I remembered and was able to do it.

Consciously chose love.

And it wasn't easy because I still felt angry, and I was still mad it had happened. I believed it had ruined my morning and I was still incredibly frustrated by this whole situation and how it was now making us all late.

Yet I did it, I chose love.

I put all the feelings I was feeling aside for a moment, knelt down on my knees to face my son. I looked him in the eyes and said,

"I know you didn't mean to do it, I know you are sorry, it was an accident. Accidents happen. Let's clean it up together."

And my son looked up at me with eyes so sad, so sorry, grabbed a hold of me, hugged me, and said,

"I love you mummy."

I wish I could tell you this is how I handle every parenting moment I have at home with my boys. And how I always choose love every single time. But the truth is I don't.

I often either forget about my commitment to choose love or I allow anger and all those other non-loving feelings to take over.

But one thing I can tell you, which I am hundred percent sure of, is how every time I do chose love in a parenting moment, it always results in peace, and the very best outcome for my sons and me.

Let's all commit when we can, when we remember, to choose love and forgiveness.

Because honestly, it really is the only choice.

Practice:

Today I want you to be on the lookout for a moment of forgiveness. A moment when you are tempted to feel angry, annoyed, disappointed, or frustrated at another person's actions, and forgive them immediately.

Their action may not have been the best choice or what you expected to be, or even right. But can you forgive them anyway?

Assuming they did what they did, not because the person wanted to hurt or upset you, but because they didn't know any better?

Love forgives. It chooses peace. And it would never allow toxic feelings of bitterness, rage, and unhealthy thoughts to fill and contaminate us.

Choose love today. And choose it by letting go, forgiving and allowing peace.

They Didn't Give Up

Choosing to love others is choosing to never give up on someone. To love them through all their times, the hard times, the good times, their pain, and even their ways.

It is choosing always to be there, support them, and love them. Even when your love is rejected, ignored, and seeming as though it's not doing a damn thing!

Because the truth is, it is. Love is always working.

And when you feel as though your love is making no difference at all, please know it is, because love is never wasted and is always felt. And will always make a difference. So whenever you ever feel like giving up and don't see the point, keep going. Keep loving.

Because I have a story.

I am an example of how love got me through. It is how my parents loved me through a time in my life when I rejected love most but needed it more.

Sometimes in life, we don't know how to help others or even if we can. And many times, we may not even be able to help, but we can always love them.

So when everything else has failed and you don't know what to do, love them. Because in all honestly, love is the only thing that heals.

As I licked the back of a postage stamp, I was reminded of a very dark time in my life. A time when there was no way I could even do such an act. Because I thought it would kill me. Or, something much worse, I thought it would make me fat.

My late teens to early twenties were such a low time in my life. I had no friends, no social life, and had completely isolated myself. The truth was I hated myself and was full of so much self-hate I wouldn't eat. I lived on only an apple a day, and when I was feeling particularly hungry and thought I couldn't go on, I had boiled some plain rice.

This went on for many years.

I lost a lot of weight, denied I ever had a problem, and fell into a deep and dark depression.

At nineteen, I worked my first real job as an office administrator, a job which would often involve doing mail outs and licking the back of postage stamps. And I remember how having once read somewhere that the back of each postage stamp contained a certain amount of calories, I refused to lick them.

I made up some lie and excuse as to why I couldn't lick them and instead used a small pot of water and my finger. I would literally dip my finger into the little pot of water and then onto the back of each stamp. A hundred times over. Crazy!

And the crazy thing, it didn't end there.

I did a whole stack of other just as crazy things to support my habit of self-hate. And as I said, it went on for years.

Looking back now, I can see why I did some of the crazy. I can see why I starved myself and refused to eat. I didn't feel worthy of nourishment or love. So subconsciously, I withheld it from my body.

I felt fat.

Or more so, I feared fat because I wasn't fat at all. I use to be, but at nineteen, I was severely underweight.

Now, in my forties, although I still have the occasional issue with body image, I am in a far better place. A place where I love, honour and respect my body (kind of like a holy matrimony except with my body).

How?

What healed me?

What got me to this place?
Love.
My mother's love through it all!

She tried her best to get me to eat, to get me out of the depression I was in, but when none of it worked, she did all she knew how to do. She loved me. And never once through it all did she stop loving me or stop telling me I was beautiful.

It took a few years to take hold, but her love eventually got me there. And I began eating.

How can I be so sure it was love that healed me you may ask?

What else could it have been!

She had tried everything else and none of it worked, and it was only when she stopped trying and began loving, did the healing begin.

Don't underestimate the power of love and the power we all have in helping others to heal. My mother, my friends, and everyone who knew me stood by me. They didn't give up. They didn't chastise me. Condemn me. Threaten or punish me. They only loved me and held me in the purest of love, and I thank them all for it.

I thank them because if they hadn't I'm not sure where I would be today.

I now lick the back of postage stamps, I eat cake, and I nourish myself. But mostly, I love myself. I know I am worthy of love, and I deserve to be loved because I was shown love.

And if there is any message in this story it is to never give up.

To not give up on that loved one. To keep loving them as my mother did me. And although it may not happen straight away, I assure you it will.

Because love heals. And love is always the answer. In everything and in all circumstances.

Practice:

Is there an area in your own life or a loved one's you are just about ready to give up on?

Maybe it's your weight or a friend who no matter how hard you try will not clean up their act. Or maybe it's a child of yours who has gone down a path you would rather not see them go down.

Can you love them?

Doing nothing at all except loving them or yourself, as you or they work through it all?

It sounds so simple and it really is. The only hard part is sticking it to it and never giving up. And no matter how hard it gets or how long it takes, to never once stop loving.

The Hug Changed Everything

I remember seeing an image of an inspirational quote once while browsing Facebook. It had said something about how beneficial hugs were and how powerfully healing they can be. At the time I must have really taken it in, because not even a week or more later I pulled out the hug. And used it as a weapon!

As a weapon of love against a war about to start.

And it worked!

Because choosing to love instead of fight, is always a step in the right direction.

Let me tell you more….

It was over nothing, a stupid little disagreement between Luke and I. Yet I could feel it, sense it was coming. The war was soon about to erupt!

I had been a bitch all morning. I'll own it. I was nagging, complaining, blaming, whining, you know, the whole deal.

Poor Luke, how does he put up with me when I get in these moods? Yet he does.

But only for so long, as he is only human after all and can only take so much before he too strikes back. And when he does, I get upset at him for being so damn rude to me, and then it starts.

The tension.

The arguing.

The war.

Thankfully we never yell or get abusive towards another, but the tension still builds, our tones change (you know the tone), and everything, which happens thereafter is anything but loving at all.

Seeing all this about to erupt and knowing it was escalating fast, out of nowhere I had somehow remembered the Facebook quote I had seen earlier in the week.

Hugging. A hug. That's it - I'll try it. That'll do it!

With all my strength (and believe me, it took some power) I stopped arguing, pushed the bad mood aside, looked Luke in the eyes, grabbed hold of him, and hugged him. And I did not let go.

And do you know what?

It absolutely changed everything.

The tension, our moods, the silly little argument, all of it, completely disappeared. I even apologised for my behavior, and together we laughed at it all. And I walked away feeling like the good guy!

But really it wasn't me.

I wasn't the better person here.

I had only stopped the war by choosing to love. Or should that be choosing to hug?

Hugs to me have since become everything. They are now my weapon of choice, because you honestly can't argue with a hug. And you certainly can never argue in a hug.

Hug it out.

Try it. Give it a go. Do it.

Next time you're about to go completely crazy and lose your cool. Hug. Especially when you don't know what else to do. Because not only does it feel damn good to do, it's one of the best ways to love someone.

Practice:

Your challenge today is to hug at least one person. Or better yet, hug someone who needs it from you. Even someone you don't know so well.

Only requirement with this one is the hug be full, significant, and extended. No quick hugs allowed. But a full intentional and loving long hug.

Enjoy this one. I'm sure you and the other person will.

Returning it Gifted Me

Choosing love, as I have said before, will not always be your first choice. In fact it may even be a choice you don't want to choose at all at times.

I have many examples of this in my own life.

Times when I didn't want to choose love because I knew by doing so it would inconvenience me or require effort on my part.

Yet as a dedicated 'love chooser' I choose it. And whenever I do, it always (and I repeat here ALWAYS) blesses me in return.

Love is a two-way street. It not only blesses the receiver but the giver too.

Let me share a recent example of this from my own life.

Gabe had forgotten his drink bottle. Again. The second time in a week!

Now I admit this can set me off and have me feeling all sorts of mad. Because it usually means one of two things.

Either one, I can be a super mean mummy and have him learn his forgetful lesson and go an entire day without his water bottle. Drinking only from the shared school bubbler at 11 am, and later at 1 pm. The only times he would be outside to use them.

Or two, go with the other option of returning home, grabbing the damn drink bottle and returning back to the school (again) to give it to him.

Guess which option I took?

The second one! People, it's always the second one.

Why?

Not because I am the best mum ever, but because the guilt of not doing it and him going without would kill me. Regret is probably my biggest weakness. It can consume me some days.

But what I loved most about my choice on this particular day was amongst my bad mood and all the anger, and amongst my having to drive all the way back home and then back to the school again. Was the gift it gave me.

The gift of turning up to Gabe's classroom 45 minutes to an hour later and seeing his whole face light up and call out to me, as though seeing me had just totally made his entire day.

Because it did!

Seeing me was such a huge surprise and gift to him.

And how good does it make you feel when you see someone completely light up at your presence or be so damn happy and delighted to see you. And I can assure you it wasn't the drink bottle Gabe was happy about, but me..

Yet, at the same time, it can also leave you feeling a slight tinge of regret and sadness as only a few moments earlier, you were cursing the damn boy for forgetting the drink bottle in the first place!

Love. It really does change everything.

Seeing love and joy in Gabe's face as he saw me melted away all the resentment and anger I had held. And all this only happened because I had chosen the loving choice, to return back to school with his drink bottle.

Love. It truly conquers everything. Let us all choose it. Not only because it is the right thing to do, but because it feels so damn good to do so.

Practice:

Be on the lookout today and in the days to come for opportunities to love others, particularly when you don't want to.

Maybe it is going out of your way for someone like I had in the story above. Or perhaps loving them will cost you your afternoon when you had plans to spend it another way.

Or maybe you don't have the time, energy, or are simply just not in the mood to love someone today.

Love them anyway.

Choose love and just do it.

Why?

Because I promise you the love you give will not only bless the person you are showing love to, but you will be blessed a thousand times more.

Choosing Love When It's Not Easy

"You're not afraid to love, you're afraid of not being loved."

I have come to realise in life that when it's the most difficult to love is when it is needed the most.

Love isn't always easy they say. Very true! But it is possible.

And the stories I share in this chapter are about such times. Times when love perhaps wasn't my first choice, but I chose it anyway.

Times when loving someone involved forgiving them, letting something go, or putting aside myself for five minutes.

Times when I knew what the loving thing to do was, and although I didn't want to do it, I did it anyway.

Love is always a choice. That is true. That I know.

But choosing it isn't always going to be easy. Sometimes it will require great force, strength, and a commitment from us.

But I know you can do it, I know it's possible. And it all starts with a simple choice here and now to choose it. To choose love no matter what, always and forever.

Will you make that commitment with me?

Will you commit to honour, and choose love every single day regardless?

If so, then welcome. Welcome to what is about to be the journey of your lifetime. Because I assure you, if you can love during the difficult and challenging times, then you can love anytime, anywhere, anyone, and everything.

And if you can do that, then you truly are one exceptional and magnificent human being.

The Commitment

It is easy to love someone when they are nice to you, helping you, and loving you back. But what about when someone isn't any of these things? When they are treating you poorly or in ways that are unloving and unkind?

Can you still love them then?

You can!

But it is often hardest.

And although it may seem hard to love others during this time, it is absolutely one hundred percent the most crucial time to love them. Because this is when our love is needed most.

So commit today, like I am, to love others who need it most. To love those who are hurting and are hard to love. To love those who may not deserve our love, but are worthy of it anyway.

Because deep down, it's these people who are crying out for love. And for whatever reason, are too afraid to ask.

I know because I have been that person.

We have all been that person.

The Kettle. The Toaster. The Morning.

One of the most difficult times to choose love is when you're mad. Especially when the person you are mad at is the exact same person you are trying to love!

I know because this is something which continues to come up and challenge me. Yet as I am committed to love, I am also committed to choosing it even when it's difficult.

But what about those times when it's really difficult? Like really, REALLY, difficult?

Do I still choose it then?

For the most part yes, yes I do.

But then, of course, there are times I don't.

And sometimes, that is the way it goes. You have to step out of love to get back into it. And the following story is about a time when, although I didn't choose love at first, it led me to later realising I must.

It happened one weekend at a time when we should be enjoying our time together as a family and a couple. Yet this one morning, let me tell you, it was anything but fun.

Instead it was filled with tension, uncomfortable, and not pleasurable at all. And wait until you hear what it was over! It was so stupid and silly.

Even now, as I reflect on it, I can see how something as trivial as this could easily cause unnecessary tension in relationships.

It all started in the kitchen. I had just woken and went straight to the kettle to mix my drink. (I went through a stage of drinking lemon in hot water every morning mixed with apple cider and cayenne pepper). It was my absolute must-do. First thing. Every morning.

Luke also makes a hot drink every morning for himself, his choice being coffee.

Now the kettle is located right next to our toaster, which Luke also every morning upon waking, places his English muffin into. So there I was, like every morning, cutting my lemon in half, squeezing it into my mug, shaking in the cayenne pepper etc.

I could see and smell Luke's muffin cooking. The toaster popped. And at the same time the kettle boiled and clicked done, and I was ready to pour the hot water into my drink.

Luke heard the click of the kettle and pop of the toaster and walked on over. There is no way we both can fit in this small space and corner. But we attempted it. So a bit of pushing occurs. Luke then comes out with ...

"You are always in my way. Can't you see I'm doing something here? Making my breakfast! Why do you always wait until I'm here to do this? Move out the way. This is my spot."

It was early, I had just woken, and I am very particular about how you start your day and the mood it leaves you in. So naturally you would think I'd choose peace and love.

I didn't.

I snapped back with the following ...

"Your spot! Your kettle! You don't own it. I'm not moving. You can wait. The only reason I didn't use the area earlier was because I was making OUR kids breakfast. Something that ISN'T selfish." (Said totally overemphasising the our and isn't).

I then backed it up with:

"I didn't see you making them breakfast. That was me; I did it. You are the one who is selfish."

Luke said more things.

I said even more.

He pointed out new ways I was selfish. I rejected them and found more for him. This argument went on for a bit until Luke poured his coffee and left. And I picked up my spicy lemon concoction and went in the other direction.

We didn't speak to each for almost an entire day after this. Over a freaking kettle and spot in the kitchen. We were actually fighting over a spot!

How stupid.

It's a kettle. A toaster. And a little corner in our huge kitchen! Yet we had allowed it to cause such tension between us. Man. How crazy is that.

And you know what?

I was glad it happened because only then could I see how crazy it all was. And after almost a day of this craziness I was finally able to realise what had gone wrong.

I hadn't chosen love.

So at a quarter to four in the afternoon I made the choice to choose it.

I went and found Luke, decided to let it all go, and apologise. And although it was not easy at the time to walk up to him and apologise for something, which in respect was his doing also, it was one hundred percent worth it.

Because the moment I did, all the non-speaking and tension between us over a kettle and stupid spot, left. And love returned.

It's not always going to be easy choosing love. Especially when by choosing it, you are forgiving someone for something which they are also accountable for. But one thing I have come to realise in my 40 plus years on this planet is … someone always has to make the first move.

Someone has to be the love maker.

The love chooser!

So why not let it be you?

Practice:

Be a love chooser!

Are you waiting for someone to make the first move in the love game? For them to forgive you, ask you on that date, or make the phone call?

I challenge you today to be the one who makes this first move towards forgiveness and love. You may not want to; it may not be comfortable. But someone has to do it. Someone has to bring the love. Why not let it be you?

Piss Urine Wee. All that.

Choosing to love others is choosing to love them regardless of their actions and despite how it may make you feel.

This has always been something which has challenged me, especially with my sons. Because as we all know, children can certainly challenge our love at times.

Don't get me wrong; we love our children. We would always love our children. But sometimes our actions in response to theirs can be very unloving.

I would love to say I never get it wrong, and I always choose love, but the truth is I don't. But I am more and more.

And in the following story I share with you all about a time when I did choose love. A time when I chose the loving response over a non-loving one by simply accepting.

Having three boys and a house full of men, our toilet always ends up smelling like a public urinal. No matter how many times I clean it. Or at least it does to me, especially in the early days when my boys were only young.

In fact I think it was Gabe, my youngest, who was most guilty and had the poorest of aim. But honestly, it never mattered who it was, it was always the same every single day. And it drove me nuts!

What am I talking about?

Urine. Wee. Everywhere but where it should be – in the toilet!

I would find it lying in a small puddle on the floor, on the toilet seat, and occasionally the walls (don't ask me how). When it would then dry and leave behind the beautiful aroma of stale urine that seemed to fill our toilet 24/7.

Most days I could let it go, accept that cleaning the toilet daily (if not hourly!) was a part of life and having little boys. But then there were other days where it just plain ticked me off, and I would get so angry and so mad, and I would lash out at them.

I clearly didn't choose love.

Then there were those other times when I did choose love. I remember one such time quite clearly.

It was like any other day when I found myself sitting on the toilet, and again that sweet beautiful aroma of urine began to waft over me. I couldn't see it (because believe me, I looked for it, in fear I might have sat in it), but I could smell it.

I felt myself beginning to get all worked up at the smell and was about to unleash some ugly yelling mummy and wrath out onto the next boy to cross my path. When I stopped.

I stopped because I heard the voice of mine, which reminds me to choose love say:

"Nicole. Some people have real problems in life. And this is yours?

"Is this ALL you have in your life to be upset, worried, and annoyed about right now?

"An unclean toilet that may need cleaning again?

"You are so blessed!

"Blessed if boys accidentally weeing on the floor every day is the main concern and issue in your life.

"People are dying Nicole.

"People are facing situations and fighting for life every single day of their lives just to survive. And here you are upset that you have a toilet to clean again. At least you have a toilet. Some people don't even have a toilet."

The voice started to get a little persistent and naggy, so I stopped listening. But I got the point. It was right.

Perspective.

Perspective puts everything in place ... including urine it seemed!

And that day, although I wish I could say I had chosen love when it was difficult, love actually chose me.

Love chose to put everything into perspective by having me see things differently, through eyes of gratitude and love for what I did have. I had healthy boys, a wonderful life and a toilet! Even if it wasn't the cleanest. I still had one. A fully functioning toilet.

Gratitude is the ultimate mood changer and one of the best tools we can ever use to steer ourselves back into love. I have been choosing love for a while now, so after a while it begins to happen naturally, and the 'voice' just appears out of nowhere at times to set you straight.

But before it did I had to choose love.

And you can too.

Choosing love is easy, it really is.

It's following it through when challenged that is the tricky part. But one of the easiest ways to do this is by choosing to look differently at whatever is causing you concern.

Bring a little gratitude in, change your perspective if you can, because I promise you, if you can do this it will completely change your life. And love will start to choose you.

The next question is, will you let it?

Practice:

Today's Practice is to find something that annoys you or something you don't like, or perhaps bothers you in some way and see if you can completely change your perspective about it.

It may be challenging at first but I can assure you it is possible. For anything!

Your car just broke down? Your mother-in law drives you crazy? Your neighbors are inconsiderate and unfriendly?

Turn it around. Switch over to gratitude and love for these things.

Be thankful you have a car and have had one for as long as you have. Grateful your car can be fixed and quickly, probably within a week, not months or years.

Your mother in law? Think of all the beautiful things she has done or does do for you. And if you cannot think of one single thing, then at least be grateful she gave birth to your husband or your wife.

The neighbors. This one can be hard if you don't know them so well. But what do they do that is loveable? Perhaps they have a wonderful garden? Watch over your home when you are away, or at the very least know they could always be worse, and be thankful they are not.

Feeling gratitude and love in situations which usually cause you frustration and pain is so much nicer. I really recommend you take the time to do this Practice, even going as far as writing it all down. Because I assure you this is one Practice if you take the time to do, will prove life-changing.

Assumptions and Judgments In The Post Office

Choosing to love others can often be giving someone the benefit of the doubt and deciding instead to let love rule your thoughts.

I have many examples of this in my own life. One I recall in particular I want to share because at the time it was challenging.

I remember I did not want to love this person because this person had done wrong by me so, why should I love her?

Because it is the loving choice and right thing to do. That's why!

But more than that, by choosing to love this person I was also choosing to love myself and not let hate, anger, or bitterness consume me and ruin the rest of my day.

Love is a choice. Always a choice. And sometimes love is choosing to believe the best of people by giving them the benefit of the doubt.

It all happened in the post office. There I was, standing in the queue, minding my own business and waiting much longer than I had wanted to post a parcel. When out of nowhere, this woman cuts right in front of me in the line.

It was my turn! I was next to be served!

But as the man called out, "Next," she walked up, taking my place and walking up to the counter to be served.

I didn't say anything. But everything inside me did!

I could feel every ounce of myself getting more and more annoyed and mad at her by the minute.

How dare she!

I'd been there longer!

And did she not notice I had a young toddler with me who was fed up with the waiting and was now roaming the shop close to losing it?

I wanted to get out of there as quick as possible, and the sooner the better. And now with her pushing ahead of me, I would be there even longer.

It was so unfair, so rude, and as I was waiting for her to finish up and leave, I felt myself getting more and more worked up and angry at this lady. I am talking like super, duper, SUPER mad now.

But then I stopped. I remembered love and thought:

"What's the point?"

"Is it really worth me getting so upset over?"

"Perhaps she didn't mean to push in or do this on purpose?"

"Maybe she didn't see me or know I was in line?

And I realised I was the one making the situation worse by playing the victim and making so many assumptions and judgments about this woman. A woman I did not know or her situation and why she had done this.

I was not choosing love and instead was choosing hate and a truck-load of dislike for some woman I didn't even know.

She left not long after I made the choice to love her and let it all go. And when she left, I noticed she didn't just walk and exit the place like an average person would, but ran out of there like there was no tomorrow.

She was obviously in a hurry. A big one

I don't know her story or why she was in such a hurry, but it was clear she needed the place in the queue that day more than I did.

But the real win at the end of the day was the moment I went from being angry, annoyed, and upset, to becoming completely ok with the situation. Seeing it for what it was, an opportunity to choose love when it is difficult to do so and actually doing it.

And I'm so glad I did.

Practice:

Next time you notice yourself becoming upset, frustrated, or annoyed at another person, see if you can catch your thoughts around this.

What is it you are telling yourself about this person?
Is it true?
Or is it just something you are assuming?
If it isn't true, or even if it is, can you let it go?
Can you choose peace and love instead?
This one can be difficult because everything in you probably does not want to love this person. But what if you decided to anyway?
What would happen if you made the choice today to love a person instead of judging them?
Give it a go and get back to me.
Because if you are anything like me, I'm sure you will find it will bring you a lot more peace than holding onto any assumptions or judgments.

The Jam Jars

Choosing to love others is also choosing to love us. Because when we are not loving others, we are generally not feeling so great ourselves!

Not loving others actually takes a lot of effort. And it requires everything that love is not - anger, resentment, blame, and numerous other feelings, which don't feel so damn good.

Although choosing to love others can be difficult, it is always worth it, even if only for your own tranquility and sense of peace.

The following is another example of a time I let it go, chose love, and moved on.

Because really what other option is there?

Stay in a non-loving place and allow whatever happened ruin your day?

No thanks!

Be a love chooser. Even when difficult.

ESPECIALLY when difficult!

Because really there is no other choice if you want to feel good!

I had been collecting and saving all our old empty jars for almost a year. Every time I would use a pasta jar, jam jar, or any jar made of glass, I would clean it, remove the label, and put it aside. I had quite a collection, which I kept in a large plastic bag inside the garage.

The reason I had been collecting so many jars was to donate to the boys' end of year school fete. I started the collection in February and it was now August. I had collected so many jars already and only had three months left to collect more.

However one fateful August morning, when I went to add another jar to my collection, I noticed the plastic bag with all my jars was missing. I searched everywhere but could not find the jars anywhere.

I called Luke at work and asked if he had seen the big plastic bag full of glass jars anywhere. To which he casually tells me he had thrown the bag out the week before!

Now here was that moment…

The moment where I could completely lose it, scream, abuse him, be mad, and have it ruin my day, week and year. Or choose otherwise.

Amazingly I chose otherwise.

I chose love!

And I chose love by deciding to look at what had happened differently from his perspective. And I realised I had never once told Luke about this bag of jars or mentioned it to him. He had no idea I was saving them.

And if anything, Luke was doing a good thing. He was trying to be helpful and noticed what he thought was a huge bag of rubbish in the garage and cleared it. Recycled it even! And that there needs applauding. Many men I know aren't so helpful.

I realised I was perhaps responsible too and partly to blame. I had never once mentioned these jars to anyone for over a year. I just dumped them there and assumed no one would touch them.

I admit every time I thought about those jars, it pained me, and I was tempted to lose it a little. And every time I thought about how many I had scrubbed, cleaned, and been saving for them all to only end up at a recycling centre, it almost killed me.

I got over it though.

By deciding not to allow those thoughts to take over and ruin me. And get this… once I started looking at it all differently, from Luke's perspective, I surprised myself by not feeling mad at him, but grateful for what he had done.

He was only trying to help, and I am glad I didn't get angry. Because what I didn't realise at the time, but realise now is, not only was Luke trying to help, he was choosing love.

Choosing to love me by clearing out old glass jars in our garage so I wouldn't have to do this.

Practice:

Think back to the last time you were mad at someone for something they did, didn't do, or should have done.

Can you change this?

Can you look at this a different way? Like I had done with Luke and jars.

Can you maybe see why they did what they did from their perspective?

And then the big challenge here… Let it go and forgive them!

Because by doing so, not only does it bring love into the situation, but it will also bring you peace. Peace by letting it all go and freeing yourself from all the anger, frustration, and pain you've been holding onto.

I Cleaned The Fitting Room

Choosing love is not always going to be easy. Sometimes it may require you to do something you don't necessarily want to do. Whether that's because it's too boring, too hard, makes you uncomfortable, or takes too much effort. There will be a reason telling you not to.

However, you can actively decide to choose love even when it's not easy. It will take some effort and commitment on your part, but you can do it. I know because I've done it and continue to do it.

The following is about a time I chose love when I didn't overly want to. Why didn't I want to choose love? Because it would take too much of my time and effort to do so!

Yet as a love chooser and someone who is committed to this path of love. I chose it.

And you know what… I felt damn better about myself afterward having chosen it than had I not done this.

This happens every time I choose love when it is hard. But, I feel I've won a battle. And in a sense, I have - against the voice telling me not to.

I love thrift shopping and looking in all those second-hand knick-knack and clothing stores. You always seem to find such great little gems and bargains at these places. I visit them seasonally or, at times, my wardrobe needs a good reboot with something antique and fabulous. And I never buy anything without first trying it on.

Because of this, I have spent many hours in a variety of fitting rooms. But there was one fitting room I will never forget. Because when I walked into this usually clear and clean change room, it was not as I would have expected. It was the complete opposite and one utter mess.

There was a mountain of empty wire clothes hangers on the floor, clothes which had been tried on and not returned lying all over the place. I even saw some gum wrappers and an empty soft drink can!

I didn't like it one bit.

It annoyed me and made me anything but comfortable. I couldn't leave and find another change room (which I wanted to do) as there was only the one and I was using it! And this too upset me. Because now I would have to stay in here, in this mess and try on my bundle of clothes amongst it all.

After trying on the first item I found myself getting more and more agitated and annoyed at the mess all around me. Then finally it clicked, and I remembered - I'm a love chooser.

Let's choose love right now, I thought. But how?

How could I turn this situation into a loving one?

I know!

I could clean it up.

Hmm, I answered back to myself. Maybe not. It would take forever, and lets be honest, I didn't want to.

But then, as I thought more and more about how much all this mess was still annoying me I realised it will most likely only annoy the next person who walks in here just as much.

That's when it happened. I swung myself back into love and decided I'd clean the damn change room.

I was having trouble motivating myself to actually do it. So, I began to think of it as a secret act of love and kindness no one would know I had done.

And you know what?

It made cleaning up the fitting room much more desirable and actually enjoyable.

I picked up all the empty hangers and placed them neatly in a pile beside the door. I folded the clothes left lying around and returned them to where they belonged – on a rack just outside the door.

And everything I didn't know what to do with or where it belonged, I returned to the clerk desk at the front of the store, leaving the change room absolutely spotless.

Now I admit, I really, and I mean **REALLY** did not want to do this, but I did it.

At first, I tried to convince myself it wasn't my job to do it, that someone else would eventually come along and do it, and how I did not have the time to do this. But what got me over the edge, and had me actually do it, was love.

Yep love.

Because the moment I thought about the next person to come into the change room and see what I saw and feel the way I did, only made me want to love them by doing this act of kindness and love.

I know I say choosing love isn't always easy, but actually it is. Choosing to love isn't the hard part at all. It is the following through and convincing yourself (and the voice which tells you not to) that isn't always easy.

But you are strong, I am strong, we are strong, and together we can all choose love.

Practice:

Today's challenge (or when you next get the opportunity) is to find something which isn't your job and do it anyway. Do it for love.

It could be picking up rubbish in a park, returning store items or shopping carts back to their original place. Or wiping down a table, collecting trays, dirty plates etc. at a local café or eatery.

Love Is Everywhere

There are many ways we can love others by helping them with something, which is their job and not ours. And what makes this all so loving is we are not doing it because it's our job and we are paid to, but because we want to. And that, my friends, is love.

Can you do it? I challenge you!

Poo

Choosing love is choosing to do the right thing, even when it's not your thing.

And in the following story I will explain further what I mean by that.

Choosing love is difficult, when by choosing it, you are choosing to do something you really do not want to do and is not yours to do.

Which is exactly what makes it love!

Because when you do something, not because it has to be done or because it is yours to do, then what other reason could there be for doing it other than love?

And when it comes to number twos (our poo) well, if it aint yours and is someone else's poo you're dealing with, then surely that oughta be love, right …?

I've been doing something for a while now, ever since I embarked on this choosing love thing. I was originally going to share the story with you all as an example of how to choose love when difficult, and how this is such a beautiful act of love and kindness.

But the more I think about it the more I don't think it is.

I think its damn common courtesy and being a decent human being!

I wonder if you will agree with me.

Now I will warn you in advance. This topic isn't the best one, or one of those warm-hearted let's love each other stories. It is gross. And probably not the nicest thing to talk or read about. But let's do it!

Out at a park one day with my youngest son Gabe I needed to go to the toilet. So off I went in search of a nearby toilet. Found one. Yay. However, as soon as I walked into the public toilet cubicle I noticed it had recently been used.

Because in it sat the biggest poo I think I've ever seen.

Just sitting there. Floating. On its lonesome! Waiting for someone to flush it.

There was a time when this would aggravate and annoy me. I would slam that door shut and find another cleaner cubicle. Now I'll admit it still ticks me off a little. But the difference now is I don't leave. I don't want to walk out the cubicle to find a cleaner one. I stay there. And I flush it.

Now people. Is this a kindness? Is this love? Or is it just plain common decency?

I'm not convinced too many people do this because I've flushed that many toilets and wiped so many toilet seats in my time, for others out there to be doing it also. Because if they were, then I wouldn't come across it so often!

Plus I have seen people.

I have stood there and watched people walk straight into one cubicle, turn around and walk straight out again and go into another. Now I am not judging you if you do this because I spent my entire life doing this! Until now. Because now I don't. I couldn't.

Why?

Love.

And because I think of the next person who will come along after me, also being exposed to the horrid sight and smell I just was.

Leave it for the cleaner? I hear many of you say.

Why? She isn't paid to do this.

You may argue with me here, but honestly, she isn't. Flushing your poo is your own responsibility. No one else's but yours. No one is paid to flush your waste down a toilet. That job there is yours.

So my hands up. I admit it.

I'm a flusher.

I flush other people's waste and wipe toilets seats free of drops of urine whenever I come across it. Not because it's my responsibility (it isn't) or because I'm a good person (although I am), but because it is the decent thing to do and I do it out of love.

Love for the next person who will use this toilet. Love for a person I do not know, never will know, or need to know. A person who I have saved from a moment of repulsion and disgust.

Love, it really is expressed in so many different ways!

Practice:

Next time you come across a dirty or unclean toilet or public bathroom I challenge you to see if you could love in this moment.

It may be picking up paper towels which have fallen out of the waste bin, wiping down the sink area that is covered in water. Or, like in my case, flushing the toilet and wiping it clean for the next person.

Or if any of the above is a little too much for you. That is ok. I understand. So maybe you could love in a different way?

You could contact the management or cleaner and let them know the room needs cleaning?

Or you could even write a letter of appreciation and thanks to the person whose job it is it maintain and clean our public restrooms?

There are many ways to love here. Choose which works best for you.

But I didn't

The following story isn't about choosing love when difficult, it's the complete opposite. It's about not choosing love and purposely holding it back from someone.

Maybe at times, you too hold back your love (and probably do so without even realising it) when the very best thing to do in these moments is to give it.

I share the following story here to help us all realise how important it is to choose love and to catch ourselves when we aren't loving.

I caught myself doing something once. Something I didn't even realise or know I did. Until I saw it! Because once I saw myself doing it I noticed how often I actually did this!

What was it?

What did I do?

Something I never thought I would do as a big lover of love and someone who vows to choose love daily in her every day.

But yep, there it was. I was holding it back. My love, refusing to give it. All because I wanted to get back at someone and hurt them when I felt they had hurt me.

I wanted them to suffer and hoped by them suffering they would experience the pain I believed they had caused me.

The most common victim of my non-love attack was, of course, Luke. I mean who else would it be? Poor guy. He really does get the worst of me. But I guess that is love (on his part to love me still, despite my ways).

Back to me not giving love and how I hold it back. The first time I noticed it happen was on one particular occasion when Luke had spoken to me rudely. Usually on a good day I'd let it go, forgive him and move on, knowing it's not me he is mad at.

But on this one morning I didn't because, for whatever reason, his frustration and anger hurt. So rather than express to him how hurt I felt and ask him to apologise, I held on to it. All of the pain, the anger, everything he had caused me to feel, I held onto, not letting it go. Yet hoping it would go away. But it didn't.

I mean does it ever? Go away?

And because I had held onto it, it only increased and made everything I was feeling worse.

So what did I do? I sought revenge later the same day.

How did I get back at him?

What did I do?

I withheld love.

Blocked the stuff.

And at every opportunity to love Luke and be kind, I wasn't. Quite the opposite. And I was consciously doing this on purpose!

Yet as life so often has it, the day gave me plenty of opportunities to love Luke. To release the pain I was holding, forgive him and let it all go.

But I didn't.

I remember hearing some really good news that day which would benefit Luke greatly. News which I would normally run straight to him and share.

But I didn't.

Instead, I kept it all to myself. And the crazy bit - I was getting joy from not telling him.

I was intentionally trying to make him suffer!

Then later something funny had happened and I remember going to tell him about it.

But I didn't.

I stopped myself and thought, "Nope. No way. I'm not sharing this with you and making you laugh and be all happy. You can suffer."

And that my friends, is me not choosing love.

I wasn't sharing it, giving it, being it, and I certainly wasn't expressing it. Instead, I was completely denying and withholding love (and conversation) from someone just to get back at them.

I am sure we've all done this at some point in our lives. Blocked our love from others or only shared it with people we like and people we feel deserve it.

But shouldn't we always love?

And shouldn't I love Luke at all times? And not only when it is convenient or when he is nice to me?

Love is committing to love another always, even when it's difficult. It is loving all of them. Yucky bits included.

Yes, we don't have to agree with, approve of, or even like the yucky parts of them or the way they can treat us. But we can still love them, the person. Not the behavior.

The same way we love our children when they are naughty. Or the same way we continue to love our dogs and cats even when they break, wreck, or dirty yet another thing.

The person. Not the behavior. That is what we love.

That is what we forgive. And this is why we choose to love.

Practice:

For this Practice I want you to see if you can find in yourself any ways you consciously withhold your love from someone.

Write them down.

Is there someone whom you do this most to in your lack of love?

Write it down.

Are there certain situations or scenarios in which you tend to withhold your love back from someone?

Write it down.

The reason I'm getting you to write it all down is because it makes it more conscious this way than just thinking about it. And when you have physically seen what you do and written it down; it will be easier to spot next time you do it. Trust me on this one.

So the challenge for you in this Practice isn't to love someone, it is to catch yourself NOT loving them. Because the more times you do, the easier it will be to see all the areas in your life you are withholding and blocking love. And then, and only then, will you be able to choose to let it all flow again.

Toothpaste

I witnessed someone shoplifting once. I did nothing. Just watched the woman do it. And as she walked away I sent her love.

I didn't know her or her circumstances or why she happened to be stealing toothpaste that day. Maybe she had an addiction to shoplifting? Or maybe, just maybe, she didn't have enough money to cover the groceries that week?

Either way, it wasn't my place to judge her, only love her. So I did it the only way I knew how. By sending her love and feeling grateful, I wasn't in her shoes needing to steal for whatever reason she had.

Choosing love certainly isn't always easy, and you won't always know the answers. There will be times when you may even question if what you have done is the right thing and if you made the right choice.

But one thing I am learning is the more times I ask my heart what the right thing to do is, the more times I get it right.

The time I saw the lady stealing toothpaste was one of those times for me when I questioned what the right thing to do in this situation was.

Should I report her? Say something? Or let it go?

I chose to let it go.

Because for me, the most loving thing I could do was not make assumptions about or judge this woman and instead send her love and pray for her.

Was it the right choice?

And would I do the same again?

Maybe, maybe not!

But it was my choice. And although not an easy one to make, I made it. Letting my heart decide what it felt was right.

I wish I could say choosing love will always be comfortable, straightforward, and clear. But the truth is it won't. And many times, like the day I saw the lady shoplifting, the choice won't always be clear, and you will have to feel into the moment. Feeling into what is right for you and the other person, and make your choice from there.

I have shared this story with you all as an example of how choosing love won't always be so fun, full of nice things and easy. Because the truth is, love will often require some not so clear choices at times. Choices in which there isn't necessarily a right one or a wrong answer, just your own.

And you have to make it.

That day I made mine. Whether it was the right choice or the wrong choice, I will never know.

But I do know I decided to choose love, and I chose it by checking into my heart and asking it what it believed was the most loving thing to do.

Practice:

Next time an opportunity arises where you are unsure how or whether to love a person, check in with your heart, and your feelings. Not your mind and what it's telling you is right or wrong, but what FEELS right to you.

Once you have felt what FEELS right to you do it and trust this is the best and only choice. Because one thing is always certain, your own peace of mind will only come by a choice you made with your heart and soul and never your head.

Bonus Practice

You may have heard of the term 'tough love' and I do believe there is such a thing. Love is sometimes doing something, which on the surface seems harsh and not so loving at all, but may in fact be the most loving thing you can do for that person.

An example of this would be reporting someone, who may be a friend or loved one, yet has done something unethical, illegal, or wrong.

Today's Practice is to think of times where you have practiced this sort of tough love. And be proud! Because it truly is one of the most challenging forms of love to commit.

I have many examples of this in my own life (mostly with my children). And also with friends and loved ones, when instead of jumping in to save them, I've stood back and let them handle it themselves. As painful and tough as this was for me to do, I did it because it was the most loving for them.

So today think about them all.

All the ways you have loved someone by being a little hard on them.

Write them down. Be proud.

And think about how this was loving them. So the next time an opportunity comes to do some tough loving yourself, it won't be so hard or difficult, because you will know the love behind it.

Broken Glass

It is a conscious choice and huge effort at times to choose love and at the same time, also choose peace. And as you all know, it's something I vow to live and practice daily.

Sometimes I nail it.

Other times I don't.

I remember this one time I practiced it perfectly...

At the other end of our house I was cleaning the bathroom when I heard a big crashing something just broke, sound coming from upstairs. It was the boys! I knew they were playing ball in the house, something I was not a fan of and had asked them repeatedly not to do.

I finished up where I was in the bathroom and walked to the kitchen. And there it was, the damage. Broken glass absolutely everywhere. The casualty - a lovely old wine glass.

What's surprising here is I wasn't mad, wasn't at all tempted to yell or blame.

I had somehow unconsciously chosen peace. And by doing so I chose love.

I calmly asked who had done it. Hugh, the eldest was dobbed in immediately and remained quiet. A sure sign it was him! So I asked him to help clean it up.

After all this was done (and for the record, a nine-year-old, or perhaps more so my nine-year-old, has no clue when it comes to cleaning) so it was pretty much up to me to clean it all up. But as I cleaned I thought to myself how peaceful the whole ordeal had been. In fact it wasn't even an ordeal!

Some may argue how will children ever learn what's right or wrong without yelling or disciplining. But you know what? My kids knew it was wrong.

They knew the moment it happened and even before it did, so what would yelling, screaming, and blaming achieve?

Nothing.

Except a horrible tension filled afternoon for us all.

And I have learnt, when you choose love by choosing peace over the yelling, freaking out, blame, and all that other yucky stuff, it is a much higher road to travel. And always results in more love, and a calmer atmosphere.

And that is the kind of day I want!

A day filled with peace, calm and good feelings for all. The kind of day I get by choosing love.

No amount of yelling and screaming or punishing the kids would ever have brought back the wine glass. So I say let it go, chose love, and move on.

Practice:

Today's challenge is to choose love by choosing peace.

Next time you find yourself in a situation that has tension, stress or tempted you to yell and lose it. Don't!

Now I know this is simpler said than done, but I assure you it is possible.

In a moment of high stress, anger or annoyance, see if you can let it go and let peace come in. Bite your tongue, clean up the mess made, or forgive the person who made a smart remark. Letting it all go, choosing peace, and therefore choosing love.

The Kind Of Mummy I Want To Be

It's only fair that after sharing about a time I had chosen peace and chosen love, I share about a time I almost didn't. And again it involves my boys and one of those parenting moments where we are faced with either choosing love or not choosing it.

Let me explain more...

What I was looking at was not poo. Though at first glance, I thought it was. It was in fact was chocolate mud cake. Stepped in, trodden on, and smeared all over the bathroom floor. It had been there for over an hour, and I had only just noticed it.

As I saw it, I felt my blood begin to boil. I looked for a child to yell at, blame, and tell how angry and mad I was and how naughty it was to do what they did.

Miraculously I stopped myself.

As the little voice of love came into my head and said,

"Really Nicole? Is it really worth yelling over and getting mad about?

"Do you think your boys purposely did this just to annoy you?"

Taking a piece of chocolate cake into the bathroom, purposely throwing it on the floor, and then jumping on it. Really?"

"What if you had accidentally done it, dropped a piece of cake onto the floor and not realised then trodden in it?"

"Would you yell at yourself and tell yourself how naughty, bad and wrong you had just been?"

Probably not!

The voice was right.

Perhaps I was really only angry at myself? Angry at myself for not watching them more closely and supervising when they ate the chocolate cake, and for not noticing it sooner.

Or maybe I was angry at myself for giving them chocolate mud cake in the first place as an afternoon snack rather than something healthier?

Either way I decided not to yell, to let the anger pass and love them instead.

Will they do it again?

Probably or maybe they won't. It doesn't really matter.

What matters more is, would my yelling and telling them how stupid they were have helped the matter or changed it?

Probably not.

So I cleaned up the mess, kept my peace, and saved my lungs a whole lot of strain and yelling. And as a result my boys spent the rest of the afternoon with a mummy who loved them and not criticised or yelled at them.

And that's the kind of mummy I want to be.

Practice:

This week be on the lookout for moments where you are tempted to lose your peace. Moments where you can feel yourself wanting to rage, blame, or say things in the heat of the moment, which you'll later regret.

Can you in these moments, catch yourself and stop? Deciding to love you instead?

Giving your own self some love and instead of pouring out rage, blame, and all those other yucky crappy things, pouring only love back in?

Can you take a breath, congratulate yourself for not reacting, and feel damn proud of you for choosing this higher road and choosing love?

This is my challenge for you. In the moments you are so tempted to lose your peace and slip into a truckload of unloving, don't. And instead, rank it up, turn it all around, and pour love back into you.

Filling yourself full of love and washing away all the unease, stress, and tension from you. Try it. It works!

I Love You Both The Same

Not sure if the following story falls into the category of choosing love, though it is about love. And about a time when my eldest son asked me one of life's most unanswerable questions.

I answered it.

Or more so, my heart answered. The only way it knew how, with love.

It was such a beautiful moment I wanted to share it in this chapter about choosing love. Because although we can make a conscious choice daily to choose love, love is never a choice. It simply just is.

Something you are, something you have, something you give, and something you could never ever measure.

I was tucking my son Hugh into bed one night when he was around six or seven when he asked me a question. A question, which I was surprised he hadn't asked up until then. He asked me who I loved more, his brother Julian, or him.

At first I answered with the typical mum response of, "I love you both the same." But then I thought about it some more and told him that it wasn't possible to love him or Julian more.

I told him love is love, and you either love someone or you don't. And you cannot love someone more than another person because love cannot be measured. Love is just love.

I explained if love could be measured and you were able to put it on a scale measuring who you loved more, then it isn't love. That is liking something or preferring one thing more than another thing.

Love is love.

You either give it, or you don't.

There is no half love, or love only a little bit, love is love. You either love or you don't.

So for me, it has never been possible to love one of my children more than another. I love them all full stop. No measure.

Yes, you could have favourites I guess, and sometimes prefer one child to another, but you can never love one more than another. Because love isn't something that has varying degrees. Love is love.

You're either loving or you're not.

In case you were curious, my answer did not satisfy Hugh that day, only confused him more. So I simply just smiled and said,

"Mum has one heart and one love. I love you all the same."

Practice:

Tell someone today you love them. No reason. No explaining. Just love them. Full stop. No measure.

Hug Hater

Choosing love isn't always easy. Yet we still choose it. And so do others. And I'll never forget the day I saw a friend of mine choose love. And she chose it when it wouldn't have been easy for her. Yet she did so for me. And I love her even more for doing so.

I had bumped into her unexpectedly while out shopping. This friend of mine. And it had been forever since I had last seen her.

So what did I do?

I do what I always do when I see someone I love or someone I haven't seen in a long time. I gather them up in one big giant Nicole love hug.

I was completely caught up in the moment and excitement of seeing her, I just had to hug her and couldn't help myself!

We chatted, caught up on old times, and promised to catch up again soon. And then when it was time to leave, I hugged her again. It was only as I walked away I remembered...

Samantha isn't a hugger. She doesn't do hugs. At all. Ever!

But that day she did.

And she received both of mine without even saying a word.

Why?

Because she chose love, even when I knew it wasn't easy for her. And she did so all for me. To love me, even if it meant feeling uncomfortable for a few moments and doing something she normally would not do.

And I'll always respect and love her more for it.

Practice:

Is there something that makes you uncomfortable?

Something which by you doing, would love and gift another?

Maybe like my friend Samantha, it's hugging? Or perhaps it's openly apologising to someone? It could be speaking up for someone? Or inviting someone into your home or driving them in a car you are embarrassed about?

Whatever it is, we all have those little things we would rather not do, yet by doing them, we are blessing another with love.

So today, I challenge you to love someone in a way in which makes you uncomfortable.

It could be telling someone out loud you love them which makes you uncomfortable?

Or maybe it is something smaller like agreeing to eat outside rather than inside, as eating out bothers you?

There are many ways we are often refusing to love someone only because it makes us uncomfortable. So today, I challenge you to overcome the discomfort and step into love.

Doing it for one reason only – love.

The Drunk Guy

You've read the previous stories about the times I chose to love others. Well, it is only fair to include a story of a time I didn't!

Oh, and how I wish I could say this is the ONLY time I have taken the road of not loving someone. But as you all know, life will challenge us, and there will be times when we don't choose love.

But what is so great about this choosing love stuff and practicing it is there will always be another opportunity to get it right and choose again. And the times you don't choose it become fewer and fewer. Believe me, they do.

I was working a double shift in a casual job I once held behind a bar when I had to practice the love I always preach. I did not pass. In fact I'm pretty sure I failed.

I'd been serving them for hours, this group of men out celebrating. There was one guy in the group who I'm not sure if he had just had one too many drinks (my guess), or if I had made an error and was confused. I feel it was probably a little of both. But according to him, I stuffed up his order. Twice.

And he was not happy.

Quite the opposite.

He was rude and spoke to me in the most condescending and manipulative way. He requested another staff member serve him, someone who was more capable of doing their job correctly. He suggested I get my hearing checked, and even went as far as to ask if I had ever worked in a bar before.

I didn't like it (or him at this point) one bit.

So what did I do?

Started treating him exactly the same way back.

I even told him this would be the last drink I was going to serve him. Ever.

This is not like me at all. And also totally against what my role requires of me. We are never to speak this way to patrons, or refuse them service without reason. But I did both!

Normally I have such a grip on my emotions. I stay strong. I choose love.

But this time I didn't.

Instead of choosing love, I chose instead to treat him the same way he had treated me.

And what did it accomplish?

Nothing.

It certainly didn't accomplish a loving working environment for myself, or peace for either one of us for the rest of my shift that day.

I could say we win some, and we lose some. But love isn't a game, it is a choice. And I am a love chooser.

Not war starter!

In my 40 years on the planet (and it has taken me this long), I have learned the most powerful and transformative weapon we can ever use is our love.

Replying angrily to this man and treating him in the same way he treated me did not help things. It only made things worse by increasing the tension.

Now, what if I had chosen love and responded to him gently with kindness and compliments galore?

Can you imagine the difference making this choice would have made!

He would have perhaps seen his own not so loving actions reflected against my loving ones, and then questioned his own. And this would have accomplished so much more than me treating him the same way he treated me. Don't you agree?

There will always be opportunities in life for us to choose again. The question is only when they come, will you choose it?

I hope so.

Practice:

Next time you are tempted to argue with someone or give someone a piece of their own medicine - don't.

Instead, see if you can love them.

Now although this can be hard and quite tricky to do at the time, I assure you the effect this will have on both you and the person involved will astonish you. It is not only one of the most powerful ways to love someone it also the most transformational.

Try it. Make it a habit. Because this here is life changing!

Choosing To Love You

"Talk to yourself like you would someone you love." – Brene Brown

Choosing to love others. Important.

Choosing to love others when not easy. Also important!

Choosing to love you … now there is something!

Do you love you?

Or should that be, do you *choose* to love you?

Because loving you is also a choice and a choice which won't always be easy. But it will always be a choice.

I wish I could say loving yourself comes naturally. And perhaps for some, it does. But for most of us I realise it does not.

Which is what makes loving you a choice. And a super important one at that.

Choosing to love you isn't only being kind to yourself or treating yourself to an expensive glass of wine (though it can be). It is often little things done in a variety of different ways - all with one single thing in common.

Love. And You. In the same sentence!

The following stories I share are about various times I or someone I know have chosen love. And by doing so were also loving themselves in the most beautiful, kindest, and compassionate of ways.

Because let's remember when it comes to love. We must never forget ourselves.

Out of Reach

Our hearts are such powerful, beautiful things, and loving them isn't always so easy. Because sometimes it hurts to feel such intense emotion. Whether the intense emotion your feeling is love, sadness, grief or joy.

Songs, I believe, are powerful and can elicit all sorts of emotion.

I often have days when an intensity of emotion can fill me. Most of the time it is either sadness or love, yet on this particular day, it was both. And what brought it all on was a song.

Let me share with you more…

I knew by clicking on it it would hurt, but I did it anyway.

It was a song I saw suggested on YouTube as next to view. I knew by opening it that it would bring up so much emotion.

The song was 'Out of Reach' by Gabrielle.

Yet, the most loving thing I could do for myself was to click on it. To experience it all again and let all the emotion wanting to come out be released. So I did. I clicked play, and as the song and its lyrics filled the room, I was reminded of her, my mother.

She loved this song. And she was no longer here to enjoy it.

The tears started as I thought of her, how much she loved the song and the life she didn't get to fully live. And as the tears began to fall, I didn't stop them, I let them.

I didn't push the memories away or change the song. No, I let it all flow and all the memories of her return as I felt each and every one.

There was a time in my life (and I admit even at times now I still do) where I just want to numb out. Blocking everything I am feeling, change my thoughts, and do anything else except feel the pain.

But this time I didn't. I felt it.

Felt it all. Because what I've come to realise is, not only is this a way to love my mother and the memory of her, but to also love myself. Allowing my heart to feel everything it is feeling. Not shutting it down and closing it off.

Because that isn't love!

Nor is it kind to me.

My heart, in moments such as these, wants to express and feel everything it is feeling; it's what she was designed to do, feel! And the most loving thing I can do is allow it to feel.

So I did.

I allowed myself to feel all I was feeling and not let the fear of feeling decide whether or not I play the song. I let love decide. And love chose to play the song. To feel it all again, be reminded of her, and to experience once more the heartache and joy of having her and then losing her.

Our hearts are such beautiful things. They want to feel. Let them!

They were designed to feel. Allow it.

Because when it comes to feelings and emotion, all our hearts want is for us to allow them to feel. And loving you is letting you be just as you are. Without judgment - being completely and fully you in each and every moment.

Practice:

Today let whatever rises be. Don't judge it. Simply just watch it, let it be, and allow yourself to feel all that is there to feel.

Don't make it wrong or right, they are only feelings arising to be felt and then let go. Like waves in the ocean, passing the moment you allow it to wash over you.

Time Well Spent

Choosing to love you will often involve choosing to ignore the voice which is trying to convince you not to. And we as women, (and perhaps some men too), seem to struggle the most. I know this is something I battle with constantly and admit, it's also the one I fail at most.

Because for whatever reason choosing to love myself tends to always come last. Right on after loving the children, my partner, others, work, friends, and even the house. The house gets more love than I do most days, it's ridiculous.

But then there are times when I do choose to love me, and when I do, it's no surprise I am a happier and much better person because of it.

We all deserve love.

You, me, everyone!

And we must never forget ourselves because that too is important. Oh so important.

I had wanted to clean. Well, actually I didn't want to - I needed to. So I did everything possible to avoid it. I do that. Avoid things. Find things to fill my time with other than the actual thing that needs doing.

On one particular day rather than clean I suggested we walk up the mountain reserve near our home as a family. I knew I was avoiding cleaning the house, but this was one time where I knew my choice (although made to avoid doing something else) was the more loving one at the time.

You see I did not want to clean the bathrooms and vacuum that day. I was only doing it because it needed to be done, and I was forcing myself to do it completely against my own will.

With every bench top wiped and room vacuumed, I was becoming more and more angry and resentful, feeling anything but love. I didn't want to clean right now. It was a beautiful Sunday afternoon and what I really wanted to do was spend time with my family having fun doing what we love. That is what I desired to do. Not clean!

So why was I cleaning?

Because I was loving the house more than myself!

And I was putting the house and its needs above my own. Yes, the house needed some love by cleaning it, but so did I.

I needed love, and I needed to stop, take a break, and spend time with my family, filling myself back up with love.

How often do we do this though?

Choose others and their needs before our own. Or choose self-made obligations and all those other various things we tell ourselves we have to do right now. Completely ignoring our own feelings and what our heart truly desires and needs?

Now I'm all for helping others and taking action. I can hear many of you probably thinking if you have this attitude the house will never get cleaned. It will!

The point I am making here is about the many times we choose to love others instead of loving ourselves. We will clean the house first, help with a friend first, volunteer our time somewhere, and only then we will find some time to love ourselves.

This isn't love. Because it ends up leaving us feeling bitter, resentful, and angry the entire time we are 'loving' these things or people. And it creates anything but love when you are coming from this kind of space. Because let's be honest, it isn't really loving the other person, house, or yourself at all.

We are much better off filling ourselves back up with love, feeling good, feeling love, and then giving ourselves and time to others and the things we promised we'd do.

Yep, even the house deserves, and I'm sure enjoys, to be cleaned by someone in a happy, loving mood versus someone who is not.

So as I walked with my family that day out in nature near our home I decided to love myself first and realised, although the bathrooms needed cleaning, they could wait.

And I asked myself if it really did matter if I cleaned the house that day or the next?

Or even in two days time?

Probably not!

As long as it gets cleaned.

And what mattered most was getting my priorities right and choosing love.

And the most loving thing I could do for myself in that moment was to spend time with my loved ones, not bathrooms.

So I chose it. Love. And loved myself by saying a big fat no to bathrooms and a great big yes to me.

Practice:

In what way can you love yourself today?

Perhaps like me in the example above, it's choosing to put aside a must do for the moment. And making YOU your must do by choosing a little self-love, time, and attention for you.

Or maybe it's simply giving yourself permission to stop, take a rest and have a break? And the permission to do something you enjoy even though something else may need doing or is pressing you for your time and attention.

Today's challenge is to simply choose you. Enjoy!

Pronioa (pro. Noy. Ya).

Choosing love for yourself is choosing to be hopeful and only wanting the best for your life. It's choosing to uplift yourself, encourage yourself, and have your own back cheering yourself on.

Love isn't only, "I love you." It's support. It's hope. It's joy. And it's a way of life. Which reminds me of a word I know.

A word which once learning the meaning of, realised is the most loving way I could ever live my life. So I began choosing it and living it. Let me explain.

There is a word I know.

Pronioa.

Although its meaning isn't quite referring to 'Love', it basically is. Because love is all this word asks of us.

The word – Pronioa, is in fact a condition.

What is it?

Basically the opposite of paranoia!

It's where you have the belief and constant feeling the whole world is out to bless you. A world which is constantly conspiring to turn everything that happens to you, to good. And a world where only good things happen to you.

Yep, pronioa I want that!

In fact I kind of already have this belief. Because I honestly do believe the world we live in is FOR us and not AGAINST us.

Trees grow to shelter us and to provide food. The rain always comes, even if it is after a long drought. A new friendship forms after a broken one, or new love is found after losing love. And then there are the little everyday examples in my own life.

Like when my employer contacted me at the last minute and told me my shift for the evening had been cancelled, along with every other shift for the remaining week. There was an administration error.

Freak out I did. Swear I did. Upset I was. As it would result in no income for a week and a complete change in all my plans but…

I let it go.

I surrendered.

And I let that little thing called Pronioa kick in.

Everything happens FOR me, not AGAINST me, I told myself. It will bless me. I told myself. And it will turn out for good I kept telling myself as I went on with my weekend.

And you know what?

It did!

The weekend, which I usually would have spent working was filled with blessings. Blessings which would not have occurred had I worked all those shifts!

A friend invited me out for dinner who insisted she pay for my meal. A dinner I would never have been able to go to if I had been working. And a dinner, which as it worked out, didn't even cost me a cent! Saving me money, money which I no longer would have had of due to my shifts being cancelled.

I was also able to watch all of my sons' football matches that weekend which I would have missed due to my shifts at work. And I was there when one of my sons scored his first ever goal.

Both of those things blessed me. They were good things.

Good things which resulted from what I first believed to be a bad thing when my employer cancelled my shifts.

Pronoia.

Yep. A little something we could all use more of, don't you think? Because let's face it, which would you rather?

Believing the world is out to get you? Or bless you?

I know which I prefer. Pronoia.

Practice:

Today or next time something unexpected happens, something you feel is a 'bad' or 'negative' thing, see if you can let a little Pronoia kick in. Choosing to see it as a blessing instead. And wait expectantly for this so called bad thing to turn into good and bless you.

I would love to hear from you and your everyday examples of how a little Pronioa turned around and blessed your day. Please feel free to get in contact with me on my Facebook page or website, and share how something you previously called bad, turned into something indeed quite wonderful xox

Feet

Choosing to love you is choosing to be kind to yourself. To treat yourself the way you would your own child, a dear friend, or someone else you deeply care about and love.

Yet do we?

I often catch myself being anything but kind to myself. This isn't love, nor is it kind, and although it will continue to happen, we can stop it by deciding to choose love instead.

This is why I am sharing this story with you. Because it is about a time when I stopped the not nice mean voice that wasn't loving me, and turned it into one that was. One of love!

It was like every other time I looked at my feet. The same thoughts repeating over and over to me, perhaps worded slightly different each time, but always to the same effect.

"Eww. Yuck. What ugly feet you have."

But this time I stopped the thought before I could let it finish.

"That's mean! That's not lov at all." I almost shouted back to myself.

Clearly, I was having a good day as I had picked up on the non love talk so quickly. Usually it would consume me and take a long time before I realised and had a chance to stop it.

But this day I caught it. And catching it I decided to turn it into love.

But how?

Perspective!

There it is, that word again. But as I have said before, it works a charm. It can turn any situation into gold. So I gave it a ago.

I looked down at my feet and this time I didn't see ugly feet, I saw two AMAZING feet.

It is amazing because lets think about our feet for a moment and what they do for us every day.

Those feet, your feet, and my apparent ugly ones have been with us ever since the day we came into this world. And let's face it, without them, we wouldn't be able to live the life we do.

They help us walk, and more importantly than that - they keep us upright!

And they were the very reason we were able to take our first steps.

They walked us into class on our first day of school, and out when we graduated.

And for many, our feet have (or perhaps will someday) walk us down the aisle.

They keep us balanced.

Allow us to jump, run, play sport and look killer sexy in a pair of heels.

Our feet are clearly amazing.

Silent wonders they are. Here only to serve us and take us wherever our heart desires.

So thank you, I said to them. Thank you, my dear sweet darling feet. You are both so fantastic and although many may class you as ugly, and on one too many occasions I have too. Without you, my life wouldn't be the same. I love you.

And, as simple as that, I had chosen to love me, and my feet. And you want to know what?

It felt damn good to do so.

Practice:

Find something about yourself that you really do not like or love. And love it!

Perhaps it's your nose?

Your thighs?

Or maybe it's your really curly hair, balding head or hair that isn't long enough!

Or perhaps it's like a friend of mine I know who has the most amazing dimples, yet she hates them.

Whatever it is, find it and love it today. And see if you can do what I did in the story above by changing how you look at it. To a new perspective. To one of love!

Alone. Alone. Alone.

Choosing to love you is choosing to treat yourself. It's choosing to spoil yourself and to do something you normally wouldn't, because it's either too extravagant, you believe it's too selfish, or you don't want to spend the money or time on yourself.

News flash here people. You are incredibly important and worthy of all the love you can give yourself.

This reminds me of one such time I made a self-loving – let's choose to love me here - choice, that I almost didn't.

It wasn't extravagant, nor was it expensive, and I had plenty of time. So it wasn't any of those things that tried to prevent me from giving myself some love.

So what was it?

I thought it was selfish.

And so I tried to convince myself it was selfish to love myself in this way and almost didn't'. Let me share more…

It was a routine day like any other. I had just dropped all my boys off at school when instead of going straight home to fix myself up some breakfast; I took myself out to breakfast. Alone!

Yep, just me, alone, sitting in a café eating breakfast by myself.

So random.

Believe me, this was random. I never do this. And if I did, I would have planned for it weeks in advance. No way would I, on the spur of the moment, continue driving straight on past the school and out to a favourite café for breakfast.

But this day I did, and man I so love that I did!

I sat alone, ordered alone, and I waited for my breakfast alone. And as this was entirely on the spur of the moment and completely unplanned, I hadn't even brought a book to keep me company. So when my breakfast arrived, I too ate that alone.

And...

It was totally divine.

Totally self indulgent.

And I loved every minute of it.

Not because I spent the time and money on myself, but because I GAVE it to myself. I had chosen to love me. And I needed it.

I remember I had had one very crazy and hectic week with the boys and the general stresses of life. So to stop and actually give myself this time and treat was the most precious gift of love I could give myself.

It wasn't easy either because when driving to have breakfast the voice in my head kept trying to convince me not to. It was telling me it was selfish and unnecessary when I could have a bowl of cereal at home or some toast.

But I did it anyway.

I chose the choice of love and ignored the voice telling me otherwise.

It was a good day. And a day I'll never forget because I had chosen to love me.

And you can too.

You can love you. You have the time.

You can spoil you, no guilt required.

You can be kind to you. You deserve it!

And you can take yourself out to breakfast just because - no reasons needed!

This is your life no one else's but yours. And it will always be your choice how you use it, spend it, and experience it.

May you always choose the choice that brings you the most happiness and love. Because honey, you deserve it!

Practice:

Look for one small way you can love yourself today. I took myself out to breakfast, but it doesn't necessarily even have to be this extravagant or big. It could be running yourself a bath in the middle of the day, eating with the best cutlery you own or drinking out of your finest crystal glasses.

It could be booking yourself in for a massage, haircut, or even just taking yourself down to your local salon, and instead of getting a haircut, ask for only the wash, massage and blow dry. Because that's the best bit, hey? Those head massages.

Today no excuses. No listening to reasons not to. Just do it. Go out there and love you. It's the only rule.

Days I fail

Choosing to love yourself is choosing to love you always.

When you fail, when you let yourself down, and even when you do something so completely stupid.

Yep. All of it. Loving you always.

Love loves, it's all love can do!

And choosing to love ourselves is something we must decide to do despite what we have or haven't done.

It's easy to love ourselves when we have done well, achieved lots, or we've been good to others. But what about the times we haven't? Or the times we didn't do anything remarkable at all?

Well, as hard as it may be, it's these times we need our own love most. And I share with you the following story of a time where I chose to love myself despite my not so excellent behavior or actions.

I had yelled at my youngest son Gabe. I can't remember exactly what he had done. All I remember from the event is how quickly I had gone from sane to completely mad.

Not a proud moment at all.

I remember there being lots of yelling to the point of almost screaming, and tears. Many, many, tears. Mostly from my dear sweet innocent little toddler.

I was over it. I do remember that.

Over the day and him! Still, it was no excuse. I love this little boy. And I am responsible for helping mould his future. And what he doesn't need is one filled with anger, fear, and my yelling. But on this particular day, that is exactly what I filled it with!

But you know what?

I forgave myself.

And I chose to love myself.

I realised we all have days like this, days when we could have done better yet, for whatever reason I didn't. We lose our cool, our patience, and do things we later regret. And sadly, as much as I dislike what I did that day, I knew it probably wouldn't be the last time it happened either.

But I still forgave myself. And I still choose to love me regardless.

It never leaves you feeling good after you have one of your moments. And we can all too easily then slip into some serious self condemnation, guilt, or regret. Neither of them is doing us any good.

But what if, in moments like these, we chose to love ourselves instead?

I did. And let me tell you, this was a much more empowered and loving choice.

And because I had chosen love to me in my moment of crazy, I forgave myself and was then able to let it all go and move forward, towards love.

I went and found my young son, apologised, and then filled him back up with as much love as I possibly could give.

No, if I had condemned myself, felt guilty, and plain terrible, I wonder if I would have given to my son as much as I did after loving and forgiving myself?

It is never right to yell at your two year old the way I did. I know this. You know this. We all know this. But there will be times, no matter how hard we try not to, we do. And it's in these moments, the moments when we are most unloving, we immediately return afterward to love.

I wish I could tell you all I have mastered this. I haven't. But I can tell you I am a lot better at it now than I used to be. And I know in a year from now I'll be even better still.

And that's all that matters.

Practice:

Next time you condemn yourself or feel guilty about something you have done, stop immediately and switch to loving you instead.

This is done by forgiving yourself and vowing to do better next time, apologizing to everyone involved (including yourself), and moving on.

Because remember love loves, forgives always, and this includes you.

I Love You Nicole. I Love You.

Do you love you?

Or do you expect others to love you? Do you feel as though it is more their responsibility to love you than your own?

And what if you had no one in your life to love you, then who would love you?

Where would your love come?

You of course!

It has to.

And it must always, even if there is someone in your life to love you.

Because giving yourself the love you need and crave is absolutely one hundred percent vital to your health and wellbeing. And not at all crazy!

But like with everything in life, it is a choice. And a choice you have to commit to making daily (if not hourly), as uncomfortable as it may be at first.

How it looks will always be different and depend on the day, situation, and, of course, you.

In the following, I share a way I chose to love myself one morning. A morning, which has since turned into many more mornings.

I share it in the hope it may inspire you to give yourself a little love in whatever way your body, heart, and soul desires today.

I had slept in again and was cranky at myself for doing so. And adding to this for some unknown reason, I also happened to wake up feeling strangely and deeply sad.

Standing in my bedroom feeling all of this, all I wanted was to be held by someone and cuddled. Yet I was alone.

This only added to my already existing feelings of sadness and loneliness. So there I was, feeling more and more sorry for myself by the minute until something happened. I remembered I could make a choice.

I could choose love in this situation, and I could choose it for myself right here and now.

So I did.

I told myself, "Hey, I'm here, and I can love you. I will love you!"

And right there and then in my bedroom I made the decision to love me. I got up and walked to the nearest mirror I could find, looked myself in the eyes and said,

"Nicole. I love you. I'm here for you and everything is going to be ok. You are so loved and held right now."

And then I gave myself my own damn cuddle!

None of the above is a lie. I kid you not. I actually did all that!

And you want to know something else?

It felt so good I've been doing it ever since.

I don't believe I'll ever stop because I need it. And let's not kid ourselves here; we all need love, especially from ourselves. And the other reason I haven't stopped since is because it felt so damn good.

I admit, at first, it wasn't easy. It was easy to make the choice to love me, but actually doing it and saying the words to myself in a mirror, and then wrapping myself up in my own arms and cuddling me…. awkward.

Like honestly, seriously, uncomfortably awkward.

But you get over it.

And when you do. Wow. Absolutely life changing.

So life changing in fact I dare you to try it.

And anyone who says you can't love and cuddle yourself is someone who clearly has never tried it.

Because if they had, they would know like I now do, just how amazing it feels to do so, and would never question it again.

Practice:

You guessed it! Today's practice is to give yourself your own big love cuddle.

Now, this is one practice I want you to commit to and do. It will be uncomfortable and a little awkward at first, but I promise you the more you do it, the easier it gets.

Whenever is convenient find a mirror (a small hand held one works fine or even try one of my quick go to favourites - the car revision mirror). Now look yourself in the eyes and say as wholeheartedly honestly as you can, "I love you."

Say it three times.

Say it as many times you need for it to sink in and for you to feel it. And then if you're feeling extra brave and bold and want a challenge - cuddle yourself.

Enjoy doing this one. You may not at first but I know you soon will.

He Bought Flowers

I want to share with you about a friend I know who told me one the most beautiful ways he chooses to love himself.

It inspired me so much and was particularly beautiful because he was a male, a bloke, a man! And what he did wasn't something most males (if any at all) would do! And it had me questioning whether my own self love was as great as his.

May his example inspire us all to love ourselves as much as he did that day.

He is a man in his late thirties, early forties. Not a close friend, but one of those friends we talk to now and then and admire from afar.

We catch up occasionally and when we do he will often share with me the most amazing tales and adventures of his life. But his latest was by far his best. And it wasn't even an adventure or a story he was sharing with me, just something he had done earlier that day.

He told how he had walked into his local florist and bought the most extravagant biggest bunch of flowers he could find, and when the florist asked him who are they for he replied,

"Myself."

He then told me how the lady had looked at him (no doubt probably with the same surprised look I was experiencing, because he – my friend, was A MAN, and he was buying flowers for himself).

Her response and complete silence when he told her the flowers were for himself shocked him a little. So he thought he'd better fill in the silence and explain,

"I'm not feeling so great today and I'm hoping these flowers will make me feel better."

He told me the lady still gave him a bizarre look as though what had said was so completely outrageous that she didn't believe him. And so he asked me if I thought it was odd for a man to buy himself flowers.

"Strange?" I replied.

"No," I almost screamed at him.

"I think it's awesome. Beautiful in fact."

It was a few years ago now, but I'll never forget it. Because, for one, I don't think I have ever done something so loving and extravagant for myself when I have felt unwell or sick. And secondly I don't think I have ever been more proud of him for doing so.

For a man who travels the world high and low on adventure after adventure, this was without a doubt the boldest, most courageous, and the most self loving thing I believe he ever has done. I applaud him.

And it made me ask when was the last time I loved myself as fiercely, boldly, and courageously as he did?

I don't think I ever have.

Until the day he told me.

Because ever since that day I have been doing the same. And I hope by doing what he did and sharing it with you all, now gives you and every other man and woman out there, permission to do so too!

Practice:

Love yourself extravagantly today. Buy yourself a bunch of flowers just because!

Pull out your favourite dress, shirt or outfit and wear it, even if you're not leaving the house today at all. Doesn't matter. Dress up. Pull out your best things. Doll up. Go all out.

Only one rule!

Love yourself. Extravagantly. In whatever way this looks to you.

Enjoy this challenge. Something tells me you will.

Saying No But Yes

Saying no. Never easy! Especially to those we love.

However, sometimes saying no to another person is the most loving thing we can do, not only for them but for ourselves.

I believe it's one of the greatest lessons in life to say no, and to say it without the guilt. And it's something I have had to learn how to do.

I admit the first few times were hard, and even now some days still are. But the guilt … Well that's beginning to fade as I've come to realise saying no is just another way of choosing love.

In the following I share with you about a time I chose it, the dreaded no. I owned it in fact! And did so all without guilt. And you can too.

I had said no to a friend whom I loved. And afterwards it started. All those feelings I often feel when I say no. Bad, guilty, selfish, and at times regret, just to name a few.

However, it was the right thing to do, I knew that. Because saying no to my friend was one hundred percent right for me. And although this no to them may not have been what they wanted to hear, it was for the best.

Saying yes when I wanted to say no would never have led to a good time for either one of us. And I know I would have later regretted saying yes and perhaps even held resentment towards this person for asking.

Or I would have been angry with myself for agreeing to go ahead with something which I did not want to do and was not right for me.

I know this because this is exactly how I used to live.

I was a people pleaser.

I was a, 'I had better say yes or I'll hurt their feelings' girl. Or if it was something I had trouble saying no to or for some reason just could not say no, I would look for any excuse, and I mean any at all (usually the kids, a conflicting event, or something entirely made up) to get me out of it.

No way to live!

And certainly no way to love!

So I decided to embrace the no. Because I realised saying no can actually at times be a way of choosing to love me.

Really you say?

Yes!

Because saying no when it is the most truthful, right, and honest thing to do will always be the right choice and bless both people.

There can be a fine line between selfishness and choosing to love you, and this is a line we must all figure out for ourselves. The day with my friend I wasn't being selfish by choosing to stay home, because I needed it. My family needed me, and I needed the time to catch up on many things I had let go of all week because of one too many 'yes's'.

And I know if I had said yes, I would have spent the whole time waiting for our fun time together to end. Just so I could get back home and back to what I had initially wanted and planned to do in the first place. That isn't being a good friend, and it certainly isn't fun.

I admit it isn't always easy saying no, especially at first. However the more you do it, the more you realise your no doesn't mean no not ever. It simply means a 'no not now'.

And this can be as much of a loving answer as a yes when we use it in a self loving and empowering way.

So own it. Be truthful. Say no to your friends, boss, kids, family, or anyone who wants something of you which you are unable to give at that moment, because it is ok to do so.

It's always ok when by saying no, you are saying one great big yes to love by choosing you.

Practice:

Today and over the next few days, I want you to be aware of every time you are saying yes when in fact, the most truthful, honest, and loving answer in the moment is a no.

I challenge you this week to say at least one no. There is only one rule to this challenge and it's a big one.

Your no must be said in love. A no that by saying it loves you or the person you are saying it to. Enjoy. And remember, no guilt! Because there will never be any guilt when your no is a no said in love.

Those Who Love You Through It

Choosing to love you is choosing to let yourself be in your entire-'ness'. And by 'ness' I mean your sadness, your happiness, your craziness, your moodiness, and your whatever it is you are in 'ness.

Loving yourself is letting you be you.

It's letting yourself feel, express, need, cry, yearn, hope, and experience all you are with love and never judgment.

Choosing to love you isn't denying yourself any of those feelings or blaming yourself when you do feel them or have felt them. It's about forgiving you, loving you, and holding the utmost compassion for yourself and all you've been through and will go through.

It's choosing to love you the way others love you.

And the following is when I allowed myself to be completely in all my 'ness', without judgment, blame, criticism or self hatred.

There I found myself again, curled up in the fetal position, twice in the same day. It was one of those days. But what I loved most about this particular occasion was how I had honored it and in doing so, had honored myself.

I felt crap. So crap. There was no hiding or escaping this. Yet, I had allowed it and allowed myself to feel this way. Reminding myself, it was ok right now to feel the way I was, and if I needed to be curled up in the fetal position crying to do so, it was ok.

I didn't try to run from the feelings or change them - I accepted them.

Why?

Because it was the most loving thing I could do.

For the first half of the day I hadn't chosen love and instead had isolated myself, too frightened I'd lash out and attack Luke or the boys if they approached me. Which they did, and which true to form, I lashed out. Twice.

But …

Eventually I chose love.

Although not at first, I did choose it!

Because I realised on this particular day I was the one who needed love most.

So after locking myself away, lashing out, and ultimately trying to escape everything I was feeling. I realised the most loving thing to do was to accept myself and feel all I was feeling.

Not change it.

But accept it.

And love me anyway.

Most days, I admit I feel pretty amazing, like super duper on top of the world great. And I put all this down to me choosing love in all I do. But then there are those days, like this particular one, when I feel so damn utterly crap. And it will happen, there is no escaping it, but when it does it too is ok.

It wasn't always this way. There was a time when I didn't think it was ok to do this. I believed and thought there was something wrong with me for feeling this way. That it wasn't ok to feel sad, down, depressed, or even angry. And I was supposed to be happy and positive all the time!

Crazy. I mean is this even possible?

I doubt it!

Moods, emotions, feelings, experiences, they are all a part of life. Coming and going in waves and sometimes like full on tsunamis.

But it is ok.

All of it, ok. Always, always ok.

Every single thing you feel is ok because you are human, and we as humans feel. And it is completely and utterly ok. And on the days when you are so deep in it, the very best thing you could ever do for yourself is to love you. By giving yourself permission to be this way. Like I had done.

Nothing was suppressed that day, nothing. I felt it all. I allowed it all. And the amazing thing I discovered was how those around me loved me anyway. And I loved them more for it.

We are all on our own journey, each going through something at one time or another. Some days we will feel it deeply, others we won't. And on the days we are deep in feeling it, we must remember love and to choose it for ourselves.

Because not only is it so wonderful to be surrounded by those who love you and those who will love you through it. There is nothing more powerful than when you are the one choosing to love yourself through.

Practice:

Give yourself permission to feel fully today. Whatever you are feeling! If you are feeling joy then feel it fully. Laugh boldly and loudly.

If you are feeling sad, then give yourself permission to cry.

If you are feeling frustrated and angry, express it. You can do this by letting out a big sigh or going into a closed room and screaming it all out.

The only rule is - whatever you are feeling, feel it fully and express it not depress it.

We Can Love Ourselves

I've shared similar stories about ways I chose to love myself, but this one I'm about to share with you all is a little different. And as you will see loving you can come in many forms.

It isn't only saying, "I love you" to yourself in front of a mirror, or wrapping yourself up in your own self made cuddle, or even taking yourself out to breakfast.

It can be something so incredibly basic and simple also, like being gentle, kind, and compassionate towards yourself.

And although I say 'simple', being this way towards ourselves isn't always so simple. However one day for me it was.

I was low on love and did what I know to do best. I chose love. And I chose it by taking myself on something as simple as a walk.

Let me share more…

I was feeling incredibly low and, for whatever reason, very unloved. I had no clue why, as nothing, in particular, had triggered it, and it seemed to have come out of nowhere. Clearly, this was just one of those days where we seem to feel things we don't necessarily want to feel but do.

So it was one of 'those days' and I felt it all day!

But then suddenly out of nowhere - it all changed.

Why?

Because I remembered love and remembered I could choose it. And mostly because I remembered that just like a child who is in pain or upset needs love, I too need love.

So I dropped what I was doing (housework, school lunches, dinner preparation, odd jobs here and there- you get the idea!), and off I went, taking myself out for some fresh air and a nice walk.

Why?

Because I knew it would make me feel better, and because in that moment it was exactly what I needed to do to love me.

I had barely been walking a minute before I noticed the most beautiful roses - pink ones. My absolute favourite!

Of all the different types of flowers there are, there they were, my favourite ones. Right there along this pathway as though they were planted and waiting just for me. So I had to, just had to do it. And I did.

I picked a couple of these gorgeous pink roses and took them home with me.

When I returned home I pulled out my most favourite vase, filled it with fresh water, and placed the roses into it. Roses that were now all mine and just for me!

The roses did more than change my mood. They reminded me how I am always loved, and no matter how dark and gloomy some days may be, that just outside my door, if I look for it, a little bit of love can always be found.

Practice:

Next time you're feeling a little low or down, take yourself out for a walk. Get some fresh air - breathe it all in and look at all the beauty and love that surrounds you.

You may, like I did in the story above, find a little keepsake and treasure on your walk and take it home with you. Placing it somewhere to remind you just outside your very own door, sunshine, beauty, and love await and will always surround you.

Part Three
Being Love

"Close your eyes. Fall in love. Stay There."

Being Open To Love

"Love Knocks. But Will You Open The Door?"

Love never leaves you it's always there. You are either open to it or you're not.

Similar to your house and home.

Sometimes you leave it for a short time and lock all the doors, but you can always return whenever you choose and re open those doors, because you have the keys.

Love is like that.

A choice. A Set of keys to your very own warehouse of love.

Love isn't something you can find or purchase, earn or gain, or even lose. It is something which is always there waiting to be used. Waiting to be entered and waiting to be unlocked with keys only you own.

And in the following stories, I share about times when others, including myself, have used those keys to unlock the store house of love we all have within us.

And my hope for you is you too discover your own set keys and begin to use them daily, unlocking all the love you have within waiting to be given.

His Story. Our Story. All our Stories

Opportunities to love can come at any time and anywhere, you simply need to be open and ready. Looking back at my pre choosing love days, I often think about all the opportunities to love I missed simply because I wasn't available to it.

An encounter with a stranger at my local store, the neighbour I passed daily on my walk or the mum at school who drops her children off the same time I do. There were so many every day opportunities to love, yet I was never open to it, simply because I thought it was too insignificant, didn't matter, or I didn't have the time.

No longer do I live this way. In fact I now treat every encounter with others not as something that isn't insignificant, but as unique amazing opportunities to love.

There is one encounter I'll never forget. A meeting, which in the past I never would have seen, all because I wasn't open to it. Yet this day, because I was open to it, I was able to love this man in a way so deeply profound.

Let me share more.

I met a man. I didn't get his name. And I was confident I would probably never see him again. And that was ok. Because the purpose of our meeting, the destiny and its fate that day, was fulfilled in the first five minutes we spoke.

He was an elderly man. Quite elderly. I'd say with no more than a few years left on this earth, if he was blessed with as much.

At first I didn't see him.

But I saw his walking stick, which was left hanging on the side of a shopping trolley. He must have forgotten it and left it behind.

I called out to this elderly man who was walking away. I knew it was his. Had to be his and it was. Because he returned ever so slowly back to me to get it.

I was in a friendly mood that day and naturally when my mood is good I'm more open to love, so I started a conversation.

And that's when it happened.

That's when this man blessed me, with his story. And what a story!

I stood outside the supermarket with this man for almost ten minutes. Just listening to whatever he wanted to share, which that day was his entire life and its story.

I didn't speak or share my own story, I just listened and witnessed this man as he spoke of old times. And that was all he wanted.

To be heard, to be seen, to share his story, and his life. And to know that his 90 something years or so on the planet had mattered. They did.

They were no longer only memories of his but now stories shared with a stranger. And I was that stranger.

His stories were now real, tangible, and had life breathed into them. They were no longer distance memories only he himself could carry and visit occasionally. No, they were real. They were witnessed and heard and shared with someone who could affirm just how real they were and continue to share them with others.

I stood there listening to this man share his life's story. A story filled with heartache and pain as he shared the loss of his first wife, who died during the birth of their first and only child. Then listening to him tell of the joy he had later in raising his only son alone and travelling around the world.

To finally hear him tell how it all had ended in true love. Where only a few decades ago in his 60's, he had relocated and found a long lost childhood sweetheart who he later married.

Sadly he told me she too had since passed away only the year before, after being happily married to each other for over 30 years.

This story.

His story.

It is all our stories.

We all suffer. We all grieve. We all lose love, find love, and we all want to know if, in the end, it mattered.

At the end of my conversation with this man, he clasped both of my hands into his, raised them to his heart, looked me in the eyes, and thanked me. He thanked me as I've never been thanked before in my entire life. So sincerely. So heartfelt.

He thanked me for listening and allowing him to share his story and relive all those memories again. And he told me how happy it made him feel to be able to share it with someone.

And then he turned around and walked away. Forever.

I needed to sit down after this. It was almost too much. This man - this dear man had just opened up his entire life to me and gifted me with a gift so precious – His life. His story. Who he was. What he was. And all he had gone through. All of it so precious and deeply intimate.

As he walked away, a feeling so strong washed over me. And I heard a voice (the voice of God maybe) But a voice that told me he was at peace now. That he could happily leave this world knowing his story mattered, knowing his life had mattered. And knowing someone had heard it, his story, and was able to witness it.

Strangers are never strangers if you open your heart to them. Often they are exactly what you need when you don't know you need it. Or it's you. And you are the one who is exactly what is needed.

Every day encounters I have come to learn, are never just ordinary. They are opportunities to open to love and experience the extraordinary. An encounter is never by chance or accident but by something orchestrated far beyond anything we could ever understand.

And the older man this day proved it to me. He showed me how when you open yourself up to others by loving them, or in some cases allowing them to love you, you are gifted beyond anything you could ever imagine.

Open your heart. Use it for what it was made for – love. And connect with others. Listen. Share. But mostly love each other. It's what we are all here for.

Practice:

At the next opportunity you get to listen to someone tell a story about their own life. Listen. Really listen. Listen fully and listen deeply. Giving your full attention and love to them as they do. Be an open space for their words and stories to land.

Nicole Chini

I Made It A Habit

Being open to love will often mean being open to the possibility of going out of your way for another. I have had many opportunities for this in my own life, so many I could never list them all.

I wish I could tell you all how I was open to and chose love, every single time. But the truth is I didn't. I didn't because I would find myself in many of these situations close off to love, all because it would require something of me I didn't want to give (usually my time). Or because I felt it would inconvenience me in some way.

Yet love will never inconvenience you, only bless you. And I want to share with you such a basic every day example of how love does exactly that. And about a time I was open to love when it wasn't so easy, as it required me to be inconvenienced.

It was a weekend and I was in Kmart picking up a few things. A few things, which, as it so often happens when I'm in Kmart, turned into a few more things. So many things I now needed a shopping trolley, so off I went to find one.

There weren't many in the store that day, but lucky for me, I had managed to snare one of the very last ones.

With my shopping cart now holding my small mountain of goods, I could happily continue to stroll through the aisles picking up more things I didn't overly need but whenever I am in Kmart feel I must have. I'm sure I'm not alone here either.

I was in the children's toy section (why I was here, I don't know. But again, Kmart does this to me). In the children's toy section, I noticed a lady juggling quite a few items just as I was a few moments earlier. As soon as I passed her she dropped one of her items which caused more to fall to the ground. And being who I am these days, I bent to pick them up.

She was older than me, possibly in her mid to late 60's, and she struggled to re adjust and get all the items she was carrying back into both hands. But she did it, and I began to walk away. My job there was done. Or so I thought…

Then there it was. The voice. The voice of love. The voice that often speaks up when there is an opportunity to love. The voice said,

"Offer her your trolley Nicole. You are almost half her age and can easily manage what you have compared to the amount she has."

At first, I tried to convince myself how this wasn't such a good idea and how I needed the trolley more than she did. But I have since learned to listen to this voice, and I also know when there is an opportunity to be kind and choose love, who am I not to choose it!

So I chose it.

I offered this lady my trolley, and she happily accepted. And I'll be honest with you, secretly I was hoping she wouldn't. I was hoping she would say something along the lines of,

"It's ok, I'll manage, you keep the trolley but how kind of you for offering."

Then I could walk away feeling good about myself for being so kind and wonderful without ever being inconvenienced.

Ha. Ha. Nope. Not this time. Life won't always let you get away with it that easily and will often set up little challenges to be open to love when it's easier not to love.

And I'll let you in on another little secret on how I stay open to love, because as you can see by what I just shared, I'm not always open to it and will look for any excuse to get out of it.

The secret?

I've made it a habit!

Not so much being 'open' to it a habit, but more so the way I open to love a habit. The secret is I put myself in the other person's shoes. And I imagine how I would feel if it were me, and I were the person who was struggling and needed help.

For example, on that day I imagined this lady was me in 30 years and how much I would appreciate someone offering me a trolley and helping me.

It honestly is that simple and it works. Try it!

Put yourself in another person's shoes and imagine they were you. And see if it encourages you as much as it does me every single time to be kinder and more open to love.

Practice:

Could you be kinder and more loving to someone today by putting yourself in their shoes, feeling what it would be like to be them?

It may be someone you know or someone you don't know. Feel what it would be like to be that person for a moment, and see if this inspires you to treat them differently. Perhaps a little kinder or loving - perhaps?

Hot Pink Lady

Being open to love is definitely just that … being open. Open to the many opportunities in your day to love someone.

It's often easiest to love our friends, neighbours, and those we know. But what about the stranger in the street or someone you just met?

What if you could love them simply by sharing a kind comment or thought you might have had about them?

Well you can - and I do it often!

I remember one of the first times I did this – I shared my thoughts and opened myself up to a stranger. And I didn't regret it either because I'll never forget the impact it had on her. Let me explain more…

Wednesday for me generally means the grocery shop. Love it or hate it, it has to be done. And I remember one particular Wednesday afternoon after finally finishing and grabbing all I needed, noticing an older woman in her mid 70's. She, like me at the time, was returning a trolley.

To be honest I couldn't help but notice her. In fact no one would miss her. She was wearing the brightest, hottest, hot pink top I think I've ever seen in my entire life. I loved it.

So I told her.

I told her because I also love wearing bright colours and notice every time others wear them. And as soon as I saw this lady in her super bright, (let me emphasise again) BRIGHT, hot pink top, I thought to myself,

"Wow. That's one seriously brightly coloured top. I love it. It's great."

There was a time in my life when I would have kept this thought to myself and never dared share it. But I've since learned any nice thought we have about another is always better shared than kept to ourselves.

I mean, why keep it to yourself when the thought could bless and gift another?

I remember the lady's response that day when I told her how much I loved her top.

I remember it because it was only then I realised what I had just done. I blessed her, and loved her. All because I had seen an opportunity and been brave enough to open up and share my kind thoughts.

When I shared my thought with her she said,

"Really? Thank you. I often worry I am too old to wear such bright colours, and I even doubted this morning about whether I should."

What are the chances!

And it was a chance, which I would have missed had I kept this thought to myself. A thought, which unbeknownst to me at the time, was exactly what this lady needed to hear.

I continued to tell her how much bright colours bring joy and warmth to others on cold dark wintery days like it was that day. And she agreed.

As we both went our separate ways, I walked away knowing I had made a difference to her day. And I hoped the next time she pulls out the bright pink top, she doesn't think twice before doing so and instead wears it proudly. All because of a simple comment a stranger had made.

A comment I decided to make by being open to love and choosing not to let fear, feeling shy, or simply because I wasn't in the mood, stop me.

Moments like this are always such great reminders that the good thoughts we have about others are never accidental or to be kept to ourselves. They are to be shared. And when they are, are such beautiful ways to love people.

Practice:

Today notice the thoughts you have about others, especially the good ones. Pick one and share it with the person you are thinking about.

Kiwi Fruit

This isn't a story about choosing love. It's about choosing a kiwi fruit!

Yet I include it here because I feel it is so relatable to how we often choose or don't choose love. And how in many situations we close ourselves off to love by simply not being open to it.

In the following I share about a time when I wasn't open to love (or more so the kiwi fruit) and how the moment I did open myself up to it, it blessed me.

For years I had told myself I didn't like it, and believed it too. I honestly thought I didn't like it, never liked it, and had somehow convinced myself never to let it pass my lips.

What am I talking about?

The kiwi fruit.

A fruit native to New Zealand but eaten very commonly in Australia and I'm sure many other nations and countries too.

I remember the morning so well. It was breakfast time, and I wanted my usual fruit salad. Not normally a problem with an array of fruits I usually have stocked in the fridge, but for some reason, on this particular morning, I was all out. All that was left was the dreaded kiwi fruit, sitting there alone in the fridge.

I ignored it.

No way was I having the kiwi fruit. I don't like kiwi fruit, I reminded myself. I'll go without. I'll have no fruit for breakfast.

This didn't make me happy. I really wanted fruit. I was craving it.

I returned to the fridge, looked at the kiwi fruit sitting there on its lonesome and thought, 'I'm desperate'!

So I cut it up, placed it in a bowl, and sat down to enjoy my one fruit only fruit salad (it was not a good morning).

But that's when it happened. Something which completely blew me away. I took one bite of the kiwi fruit, and the most amazing taste sensation filled my entire being.

Surely not!

Not the kiwi fruit?

So I took another bite and there it was again. Pure deliciousness exploding in my mouth!

And it continued until I had eaten the whole thing. I had to try it again to see if this was a once off, so later that day, I went out and bought some more kiwi fruits to try the following morning.

And yep again, LOVED it. Not just loved it, but damn well freaking was falling in love with it.

Where has Kiwi fruit been all my life!!!

I'll tell you where.

Right on my 'I don't like it' list, along with many other things I'd placed on some absurd crazy list. Such as the 'it's not good for me' and 'it will go straight to my thighs' list. Like will it? Really? Go directly to my thighs?

Untrue!

Lies!

Completely false stories I've told and convinced myself were true.

What a great lesson the whole kiwi fruit experience was for me that day. It honestly changed me. Because I've now realised how many of my own beliefs, stories, and all the things we tell ourselves restrict us. And for the most part probably aren't even true!

For years I believed the voice in my head telling me I didn't like Kiwi fruit. Never once did I challenge it or taste the darn fruit to see if what I had told myself was true. I just believed it.

The mind.

So powerful!

But at the end of the day, it's us who has the power. And we who have the choice. We are all holders of the power to choose. Not our minds, not others, and certainly not our fears. But us!

And although it was only a kiwi fruit I had told myself for years I didn't like, I wonder, what else in life have I convinced myself to avoid from fear of not enjoying it?

How many times in life have I chosen not to love someone or something because my mind and voice in my head told me not to?

Telling me it wasn't a good time - it would cost too much, take too much time, or even the person in question didn't deserve it.

So I say let's all choose to try things we are afraid we may not like, because choosing them may be one of the greatest choices you make. Especially when what you are choosing is love, even when you're afraid.

Practice:

Is there a food you've always wanted to try but haven't? Or a food you've convinced yourself you do not like? Or maybe there is a food you didn't enjoy as a child and therefore now avoid it.

Today's challenge is to go out there and try it again!

Being open to the possibility, you could in fact love it. And if you don't love it, then love yourself for being brave enough to try it.

Love is brave. Love dares. And love doesn't give up or give in. It tries and tries again.

You Have An Amazing Voice

Being open to love requires you to look for the moments in life when you or another person aren't open to love. And when you find such moments, do something.

Doing whatever you can at the time to open yourself back up to love and back to the highest and most fantastic place to be – in love!

Not in love with yourself, another person, or even a situation, but in love with life itself! Because when you are in love with life nothing gets in your way. You become a love machine so powerful, so full of life, and so full of love you become almost unstoppable.

In the following story, I share about a time I saw an opportunity to open up another person to love. A person who, for whatever reason, was not feeling open to it at all. Until love came along and changed all that. Here is how it happened...

I had gone to breakfast with a friend. We had a lovely time. But what wasn't so lovely was the lady who took our order.

I had noticed an attitude' about her. She spoke to the people before us in the line - very frustrated, rushed, and rude. It was obvious she wasn't happy, or perhaps it was just her job that made her that way. Whatever it was, she was anything but hospitable.

Before us others may not have noticed the not so friendly way she was taking their orders and directing them to their table. But I had noticed it, because I had worked in hospitality previously.

So when it came my turn to order I thought to myself,

What can I do to make her day?

How can I appreciate her and make her smile?

And how can I be open to love in this moment and inject a little of it into her? Because quite frankly, she could use some!

But there was a problem.

I had nothing. Absolutely nothing. And had no idea how exactly I could do this.

It was almost our time to order, and I was struggling to think of ways to bless this woman, or a way I could compliment her, because at this point, I couldn't see one single positive thing about her.

But surely there must be something? Something I can sincerely compliment her on.

Then there it was and I knew instantly. Or more so, heard it instantly. It was her voice.

She had the most incredibly well spoken and clear voice. It was so good. Like incredibly good. Professionally good! As though she belonged on a radio programme or in a stadium making major announcements. That kind of level good.

I had it. That was it.

And this was exactly what I would compliment her on!

So when it came my time to order, I waited until she had finished taking my order (which I might add she did while giving me the same unfriendly attitude she had given the previous customers before me). And then I laid it on her. I complimented her. I said,

"I hope you don't me saying this, but you have one of the nicest voices I think I have ever heard. Your voice is so clear, strong yet soft, and you speak so well. Your voice honestly sounds so professional. What a gift you have."

And right there and then. In a fraction of a moment, and with words which took me less than a minute to say, everything changed.

She smiled (the first time that morning I had seen her do so), and she completely lit up. Her whole face, posture, and everything about her was now different. She was standing taller, more open, and dare I say, even more loving. Her whole attitude and mood had changed.

And get this, the customer behind me in line received a totally different lady and different kind of service to the one I and the people before me had. A happier one. And all because of something I did. Something so incredibly simple!

There was a time in my life when I would never have been able to do this sort of thing. It would have been too embarrassing or uncomfortable for me, or just too much effort.

But not now. Now I must!

Why?

Because I am open to love.

And I choose love, want love, live love, breathe love, and I share it because I also want others to experience this love too.

We all have the capability to be at our best in every moment. And sometimes to be at our best we simply need another person to come along and gently remind us we are not.

Someone who, with only a few words and a compliment, can lift us back up and back into love again. Like I had with the lady at breakfast.

Practice:

Today, be on the look out for someone who needs a love boost and give it to them.

Your challenge is to infuse love back into the life of someone who needs it.

How you do this will depend on the situation and the person.

Some people may need a compliment or two and some cheering up. While others may need a little more, like you offering to take them out for the day, look after their children, or do their ironing.

I'll leave what you do and how you do it up to you to decide. The only rule is to refill them with love in whatever way you can. Have fun!

It's Not My Job!

I often wonder … do others do this?

Would others do this?

Or is it only me?

I'm sure others have, and maybe you have once too. And perhaps it was only me who, up until recently, never would do such a thing.

I mean, it is someone else's job isn't it?

Until love entered my life and it became mine.

This new love job of mine has even taken me into public toilets. Yes toilets, and all those 'not so nice' places.

Because being open to love is being open in all places and at all times. And this also includes time spent in public restrooms!

In the following, I share with you all about a time I was surprisingly open to love in a public toilet when I know for a fact in the past I likely wouldn't have been.

I'm a big user of public restrooms. Not by choice, I might add, or because I really enjoy using them, but because I tend to need to go a lot. And there is nothing worse when you enter the cubicle, sit down, begin your business, and you notice there is NO toilet paper.

However one particular day I encountered a totally different scenario…

There was toilet paper in the cubicle – yay! But it wasn't where it was supposed to be. Instead it was just sitting there, balancing, on top of the big round canister in which it was to be inserted. It became evident that previous to me entering, there was no toilet paper, and someone had quickly grabbed the replacement roll and just thrown it in there.

Now I could have grabbed my few squares done my business, and left. Returning the big round roll to the top of the canister like many others before me I'm sure had. And I was about to when I heard the voice of love say,

"Nicole. You can choose love right now. You can be the one to do it!" and it went on further to say,

"Why don't you replace the toilet paper into the canister?"

So I did.

And I did it because it was the RIGHT and KIND thing to do. But mostly I did it because I thought of the next person to come along after me. I thought how they like me would much prefer this big beast of a roll (like honestly, it was the most massive heaviest roll of toilet paper I had ever seen in my life – think the size of a small car tyre!). Anyway, I'm sure most people would much prefer this big beast of toilet paper in its canister than on top of it.

"Do unto others as you would have them do unto you."

We all know the saying, yet do we live it?

I personally am trying to live this way more and more each day by being open to love as often as possible, even if it is something as small and insignificant as placing toilet paper in its rightful place.

It all counts; it all matters. And at the end of the day, it's all love. Because love does that! Love not only replaces the toilet paper but inserts it too.

Practice

Next time you're in a public restroom, look for a way you can add some love. It might be picking up some paper towel that has fallen out of a waste bin, wiping over the sink area, or even placing a cup of fresh flowers in the restroom for others to enjoy.

I know this one isn't the nicest of love acts to do, but love doesn't discriminate. Love loves in all areas and in all places.

And if the public restrooms you frequently visit are clean and tidy, then perhaps leave a note of love thanking the person who kept it this way.

The Shredded Pork Bun

When you are open to love, I absolutely promise you there will always be an opportunity to practice it. I'm confident it isn't just me either, as though I have some special gift and power which draws people in need of help or love to me. Nope, not at all.

Because quite frankly, there is a whole world out there full of people in need of love and a little extra help.

Some days loving someone is simple, so simple you hardly even realise you're doing it. And you may even have trouble calling it love.

Like in the example and story I'm about to share with you.

It was so every day simple and nothing much at all really, I almost didn't see it. And it was only because I was open to love that I saw it, when perhaps I would have kept on walking, minding my own business and assuming what was calling me to love, wasn't love at all.

But it was.

Because love is often very simple!

So simple, so every day, and so easy, which makes me question why aren't we doing it more often?

I saw her standing there. In the supermarket refrigerated section. For a ridiculous amount of time, far too long that it had me curious.

What was she looking at?

What had caught her attention and captivated her so much?

Curiosity got the better of me so I walked over to where she was standing and had a look.

A 'Shredded Pork Bun Meal Kit'. A do it yourself one.

"That's new," I thought. As I had never seen this kit before in the store.

I continued to watch as the lady began digging into her handbag and pulled out one of the biggest magnifying glasses I think I have ever seen in my whole life! As in Sherlock Holmes style, one on a big stick handle.

"Oh she can't read it," I realised.

I stood there and continued watching her. And that's when I heard it. You know, the voice in me that reminds me to love and do the right thing.

It told me to help her.

But I argued back saying,

"No. I won't offer to help. It will only embarrass her, and she the lady is ok now anyway. She has the world's biggest magnifying glass helping her."

And I stood there some more - just watching.

But the voice came back (as it always does).

"Help her Nicole. Don't be embarrassed. Just do it. Offer your help."

So I did. And she accepted.

I read out loud to her everything she had asked me to, which was every single thing written on the box. I'm talking the ENTIRE box and EVERY single word written.

I read out the ingredients, the instructions on how to cook it, the nutritional value, where it was made. Everything!

And she was grateful.

So grateful, but she didn't end up buying it. But she was grateful to me for taking the time to read it all to her.

And it doesn't really matter does it? That she didn't buy it?

Because I walked away knowing I had helped someone. Knowing it wasn't a waste of my time when the time spent was helping and loving another person.

I had made the right choice. And I felt good about it, good I hadn't ignored the opportunity to love, and grateful I had listened to the voice of mine asking me to love.

And who knows, maybe I gave this lady hope, reminding her people in this world still care. Reminding her she was important, she mattered, and was loved. So loved that a stranger took time out of their day to help her.

And that stranger was me.

At The me who at first didn't want to but did. The me who remembered we are all here to love, be loved, and give love whenever we can by simply being open to it.

Because love is all that matters.

Practice:

Today, be on the look out for an opportunity to love someone by offering them help in some way. Perhaps you see a young mum who is struggling to get her bags, toddler, baby, and pram into her car, and you offer to help?

Or maybe it's helping a young child tie their shoelaces. Or, a co-worker reach the top shelf because they aren't tall enough to do so.

The only rule with this one. Be on the lookout!

Because I assure you the moment you look for an opportunity to help another, is the moment you'll see one. They are everywhere.

The Letter

Being open to love is being open to feeling things you may not necessarily want to feel. It's being open to the possibility of doing something which, although you may not want to do, is the right thing to do.

I remember not too long into my own 'love' journey realising something I needed to do. Something that a part of me still wasn't ready to do, and if I'm honest, feared doing. Yet I knew it was the right thing to do.

So I did it. Because my heart needed it!

I'm talking about our ex's and past loves. And I'm talking about letting them go.

We all have them - past relationships, past lovers. And people in our life who we need to forgive (or, in my case, ask forgiveness).

And in the following, I share about the time I opened myself back up to love by feeling all the feelings I didn't necessarily want to feel and saying things I didn't necessarily want to say but needed to.

It was unplanned, but no doubt destined I had written the letter to my ex. I had searched (ok, let's be honest, Facebook stalked) his details online, sat down and wrote. Thanking him for all he gave me and taught me during our time together.

Why did I do this?

Because mostly I wanted his forgiveness!

I wanted to be free from the guilt, which has haunted me since our break up. I needed to apologise to him for the way I had treated him all those years ago.

I was young, we both were, so young, and we didn't know then what we both know now. I also wasn't who I am today. I didn't live love, and I certainly didn't act it either.

He did.

He lived love.

Because he treated me like a queen when all I did was criticise, abuse, take advantage of, and treat him everything but what he so lovingly deserved.

It's a long story that relationship. But a relationship I am ever so grateful for and one I will always remember. Because in hindsight, it taught me so much about myself, things I never would have known had I not lived them out with him.

I don't know if he ever did receive the letter because even to this day, I haven't heard back from him. And it doesn't matter, what matters is I wrote the letter.

What matters is I let myself feel everything I needed to feel and say everything I needed to say. I let it all go, and by letting it all go, I was then able to open myself back up to love.

For many years since we broke up I had been anything but loving to myself all because of how I had treated this young boy, now a man in our relationship. And it was time to let it all go, ask for his forgiveness, and move on. And whether I received his forgiveness or not didn't matter; what mattered is I now chose to forgive myself.

Because honestly, this is what is most important here. Forgiving and loving ourselves!

Being open to love is being open to letting all that is blocking love go. It is feeling and sometimes reliving the yucky, challenging, and painful times, so we can fully forgive ourselves and move back into loving again.

Writing the letter was so powerful that night, I'll never forget it. There were tears, many tears, but mostly, it was the way I felt afterward I remember most. Free.

Practice:

Is there something in your life you need to forgive yourself for and let go to let love in?

Perhaps there is someone in your life like in mine, you never apologised to and could today?

It may be from a very long time ago, and you may not even remember the person's name, situation, or what happened exactly. Only how you felt and still do now. Great! This is all you need to do.

For this practice there is only one rule - you express it.

Writing it out in a letter is most likely easier. However if you prefer contacting the person, doing this face to face or expressing it in another form, that too is fine.

The main goal here is to let it go so you can let love in.

I want to say enjoy this one. But I'll be honest; this one isn't so enjoyable to do. The joy comes afterward when you have released yourself from all the pain you have kept inside.

Withholding Love

Being open to love is continuing to remember why you want to be available to love in the first place.

For me, it's because love feels so damn good. The immense joy you get every time you receive love from others or give it is the main reason why I choose it again and again.

Yet there still are times I don't choose it. I do the opposite. I purposely withhold it.

Being open to love requires you to catch yourself when you're not open to it. And this, I'm afraid, is often quite tricky.

Tricky because we don't realise we aren't open to love, or we have a damn good reason not to be and justify it!

The following is when I caught myself not being open to love and what I did to turn the situation around and bring myself back into being open to love again.

I had been reading about it. Perhaps this is what brought it to my awareness that day. What am I talking about? Oh, just a little thing called - withholding love. And the moment I read about it, I remember thinking to myself,

"Nope. Not me. Never. I don't, WOULDN'T do that."

Then I caught myself doing it.

Me the 'giver of love', me the 'I'm even writing a book about being love'.

To sum up quickly, withholding love is intentionally choosing not to love someone or act loving towards them for whatever reason you are convincing yourself not to.

For me, I caught myself doing it because I wanted to get back at someone. I wanted to hurt them, make them suffer, and feel the pain I believe they had caused me.

I did this by choosing a variety of ways and tactics very familiar to me. My most used and favourite of them all - the silent treatment. Then there was not sharing my joy and happy moments with them, not laughing at their jokes, and a must-do when I'm withholding love from someone - avoid all eye contact!

The 'someone' this day was Luke (and in all honesty, usually is). You see, he had spoken to me earlier this same day rudely and not nice at all. Occasionally he does this, and usually, I shrug it off and forgive him as I know it's not me he is angry or upset with.

On this particular morning, it happened to be lost wristbands our boys had lost he was upset about. Wristbands that the resort we were staying in at the time issued and if lost, cost you a lot of money.

Normally I'm good with this sort of thing.

Normally I understand it's not me, practice some unconditional love, forgive him and walk off thinking nothing more of it ever again. But on this particular morning, I didn't.

This morning I had held onto it and his words, and later, when I heard some good news, which was for him and would benefit him, I didn't tell him. And I was getting joy from not telling him. I was going to make him suffer!

Later this same day, when something funny happened, I went to tell Luke and share as I usually would. But I caught myself thinking, "No. I'm not sharing this with you and making you happy. No way! Not after the way you spoke to me earlier this morning. I'll get you back!"

And that there my friends is not only mean. It's withholding love.

I'm sure we all do this at times.

We block our love or only share it with people we like and people we feel deserve our love. But shouldn't I love Luke always? Not only when it's convenient or when he is nice to me?

Isn't this what marriage and relationships are about? Loving the person always.

Love loves another through their darkness back into their light. And it loves ALL of them. Yucky bits included.

Now we don't have to agree with, approve of, or even like the yucky parts. But we can still love the person. Not the behavior.

The same way we love our children when they are naughty or the same way we continue to love our dogs and cats when they break, wreck, or dirty yet another thing. The person. Not the behavior. That is what we love. That is what we forgive.

Yet like all things in life, we learn and we grow.

There will be times when we get it right, are open to love, forgive, move on, and love each other. And the other times - well, we need to get back up, dust ourselves off and start again.

Practice:

Be on the lookout for times in your own life when you have or do withhold love. How do you do this? What methods and ways do you withhold your love from others?

Next time it happens, see if you can turn back towards love.

Maths Class

There are many opportunities to love when you're open to it. And sometimes, those opportunities can be hidden in the mundane. Such as in our everyday conversations with others or in observing them.

I remember such an experience with my children. When I caught a moment in a conversation between them in which they were both being far from loving. And because I was open to love, I was able to then guide them back to it.

Being open to love is being open to opportunities to share it, express it, be it, and even in some cases, guide others to it.

For me, it was a day I walked into the kitchen and on overhearing a conversation between my young sons, I was given a great opportunity of parenting, and an opportunity to open another person's heart to love.

"Hannah in my class is so bad at Maths. She is the worst in the whole grade. She can't even do times tables, and she's in year 3!"

I overheard my eldest son Hugh telling his younger brother Julian while they were eating lunch.

"How do you think Hannah feels about that?" I asked them both.

I went on further to say,

"It must be hard for her not being able to do what all the other kids in her class can. She probably wants to be good at Maths like you and all the other kids. Don't you think?

"And I wonder how it makes her feel not being very good at it?"

And then I walked out of the room.

I didn't say anymore or even give them an opportunity to respond. I left purposely at that precise moment in the hope of giving my boys a little something to ponder.

Compassion. Love. And seeing life through the eyes of another!

I'm not sure if my conversations with my sons ever did that day open their hearts to love or to compassion. Or if it had them seeing life through the eyes of Hannah. As compassion and love isn't something, we can teach our children, only display.

I feel so strongly against putting others down only to raise yourself. So when I see it in my children, I do all I can to stop it.

I don't do this forcefully or by reprimand, but by giving them another perspective. And by doing so, hopefully opening my children back up to love.

This sort of thing often happens in our home. I will suggest a different way of looking at things in the hope it will help my boys to walk in the way of love.

Because in all honestly, that is all we can ever do.

You cannot make someone love, nor can you make another person open to love, but you can guide them to it. You can open yourself up to love and, by being so open, inspire them to be.

As a mother I live this way. Open to love always and as often as possible.

My eldest is now in his teenage years, and his brothers soon to be, and over the years I have seen them all opening more and more to love.

And why?

I like to believe it was because it was demonstrated. Because as young children they were ever so softly and gently guided to it, by someone who themselves was open to love.

And that person was me.

Is it you?

Practice:

Is there a way in your every day conversations you could steer another towards love?

Perhaps it's when you notice someone gossiping about another person or sharing information that isn't so kind or even necessarily true?

Is there a way you could guide them to a different perspective? One geared more towards love?

Look today and in all your future conversations for opportunities to turn unloving ones back to love.

Note: I admit this one may be hard to spot and notice at first, and even a little tricky to master without coming across as bossy and judgmental. But I assure you it can be done. And with practice, every conversation can be steered back towards love.

Interrupted

I'm not always open to love. And when I'm not it's never fun and quite frankly sucks.

And the worst part is, most of the time you don't even realise you're not open to it.

And it's not usually until someone comes along and either tells you you're not (which, let's be honest, isn't always the nicest to hear). Or someone comes along and displays how open they are to love, snapping you out of your unopened state and inspiring you into an open one.

I have had many times in my own life when I have been closed to love, not even realizing it until someone has come along who was so open, so joyfully happy, expressing love, feeling love, and just generally having a damn well better time than me. That I realised - hang on a minute, where is my love?

The following is about a time when I was closed to love, yet my son wasn't. And how this encounter with my son - although it didn't inspire me to open to love in this particular moment, it did change me.

It changed me because it showed me just how living openly to love is done.

Every morning I like to do a little yoga. I find stretching my body not long after I wake up always feels good, so good. And it helps me wake up.

It's become almost ritual, a must do every single morning. So when I don't do it, I feel well, yuck, angry and disappointed I didn't make the effort.

One particular morning I remember while doing my morning stretches and yoga, my youngest son Gabe walked into the room.

I said my usual good morning, asked if he was ok (he was) then smiled at him and continued doing my morning stretches.

I thought he'd leave. And in truth, hoped at this point he would. Because he was disrupting my routine and I was beginning to get annoyed at him just standing there in the doorway staring at me. It was distracting and disruptive.

I looked at him again, wondering why the heck he was still standing there, and that's when Gabe finally made his move.

He approached me mid yoga pose, wrapped his little toddler arms and body around me and gave me the biggest cuddle a boy of his age could, and said, "I love you mummy," and left.

I wish I could say my heart melted at this point. I wish I could tell you I stopped, grabbed Gabe into my arms, and cuddled him back.

But the truth is I didn't.

Recalling it now, and each time I do, my heart swells and melts, and then I feel remorseful. But at the time, I have to admit, my heart didn't melt, nor was I filled with remorse of any kind. I was just plain annoyed. And happy he had left.

Why?

Because my heart was closed to love. And sadly, only open to yoga!

It wasn't until after he had left I realised just how closed I had been. And how open he had been. And I love that about children.

How open they always are to love. How no matter what time of day or mood you or they are in, they always find little ways to express themselves in love. They will say what they feel, ask for what they want, and generally don't give a damn how it looks or what you or others will think of their love. They just give it.

Like my son Gabe had by interrupting me just to say, "Mum I love you", which in actual fact was not an interruption, only I had made it one!

How many adults do you know who would do that?

Walk up to a person, express their love and then simply walk away, not expecting anything in return?

Not too many.

But children and those open to love do it all the time!

Gabe was open to love. So wide open he couldn't contain it and had to express it. And no yoga, closed door, or mum's mood was going to stop him.

And that is how you live love openly.

Bless my beautiful boy for the lesson he gave me. A lesson, which almost six years later, has still stayed with me and changed me ever since.

The lesson?

Love stops no one.

Practice:

Let love guide you today don't let your thoughts, mood, or others stop you. And if you're feeling really bold, I challenge you (like my young son had) to walk up to someone you love and say, "I love you", turn around and walk away.

Don't look back and certainly don't expect or await a response in return. You are gifting them with your love remember?

Enjoy!

Making The Call

Being open to love a lot of the time may mean putting yourself in situations you find uncomfortable.

I have many examples in my own life where I have sadly chosen comfort over love. Choosing my ego and pride instead over forgiveness, saying sorry, or I love you.

Yet of all these times, which are all different and unique to each other, one thing remains the same. I never feel good afterward. Because not only have I denied another person my love, but I had denied myself.

But we live, we learn, we experience, and each time we get better and better at choosing love and being open to it, even when it's hard.

I want to share with you all about a time when, although I did not want to open to love, I did. And even though it was scary, uncomfortable and made me feel vulnerable, I still did it. Because I knew it was the right thing to do.

And guess what?

It has made choosing love when vulnerable, uncomfortable and scary. But the only way for it to ever get easier is to step right in when it's not.

Let me share a little more …

When my eldest son Hugh was younger he had a play date. It was his first real 'big boy' playdate and he had been anticipating it all week. You see, he loved this boy. Like really, REALLY, liked him.

As a person who knows all about opening to love and being open to love, I had to venture a little out of my comfort zone and do something I didn't want to do - contact the boy's mother.

I didn't know her. She didn't know me. And well it was awkward. So I put it off. For months in fact!

Hugh had given me the number at the beginning of the school term, and I had put it aside in my drawer with the "maybe he'll forget he ever gave it to me" pile. Because I really (and I mean really) did not want to call this woman. I mean, how awkward.

The whole 'you don't know me, I don't even know if you know I have your number, but your son gave it to my son, and my son gave it to me' was awkward, uncomfortable and something I struggle with!

I was also convinced this kid did not like Hugh or want to hang with him because I had heard from his brother this kid was the 'coolest' kid in class and Hugh, well, wasn't, and idolised the boy.

But you know what I did it. I called.

Because sometimes in life (read: most times) it isn't always about you and your discomforts. It's about the most loving thing to do in the moment, the *right* thing to do. And calling her was. Not for me, but for my son and this boy I did not know.

I still, at times, struggle with this one. I want to play it safe, I want to feel comfortable, and I avoid making such calls. But as I am learning more and more to be open to love, I have started making these types of phone calls. I put myself out there, and yes, it feels vulnerable.

But you know what?

Every single time I do it, I am grateful because the majority of the time it blesses me. Or as it so happens on that day, blesses two young boys who, had I not made the call, would never have developed and begun a friendship which was to last many years.

It made me question and think of all the connections I may have lost over the years, all because I was too damn scared to put myself out there and say hello or call.

Not anymore.

No.

Now I bravely and boldly take the risk. I choose to be open. Open to friendships, open to love, and of course, willing to being vulnerable.

Practice:

In what way could you put yourself 'out there' today?

Perhaps there is something you have been putting off from fear of rejection, embarrassment, or lack of confidence?

I challenge you today to be open, to make the call, say hello, do what it is you have been putting off for what seems like forever perhaps because of fear.

Because love doesn't allow fear to rule the heart. Dive deep into your heart today, and see what it is craving, what it desires but is too scared to do – and then do it. Do it today. Because if not today then when?

I Accepted Him

Being open to love is being open to accepting people for who they are and loving them anyway. And believe me, this one isn't always so easy!

Now I'm not saying here that we should tolerate another person's disrespect, abuse, or any other behavior that clearly is not to be accepted. No, not at all! I am simply saying that we can still always choose love and be open to it, despite how another's actions may irritate us.

And the following is about a time I made the decision to let go of my expectations as to how a person should or shouldn't behave and just love them anyway.

Of all my sons Hugh, the eldest, can frustrate me most. It's always been this way and it's always been him.

As a toddler and young boy, Hugh would go off with the 'fairies', not listening, not fully present, in his own world, and ever so slow at responding to anything. And let's not forget his attention span or his listening. It just never happened. Ever. Frustrating. So frustrating!

Even now, with Hugh in his teen years, it's much the same. Yet now added to this are other little 'quirks' of his which I find can irritate and frustrate me. And it's these little 'quirks' and behaviors, that have me guilty of closing to love rather than opening to it.

One morning many years ago I realised this was no way to live. I couldn't be an advocate for love and out there preaching it, if every time my own son frustrated me, I closed off to love and reacted back.

I remember a day when Hugh had ignored something I had asked him to do. He was off in his own world, spinning a fork on a table non-stop, trying to get it to balance. And it was driving me nuts.

I could feel myself starting to boil inside. You know the feeling. Where every single sound and scrape of the fork (or whatever it is that is irritating you) is driving you more and more crazy by the second. And you feel like you are about to explode.

Well I was about to!

And I wasn't sure I could keep it in any longer. I wanted to yell at him and tell him to stop doing what he was doing. I wanted to tell him how wrong it was and how most little boys don't do this.

None of this was true, of course, and the truth was I only wanted him to stop and look at me while I was talking to him, and quit playing games. And to stop making the irritating sound of scrapping metal.

I also wanted eye contact, a nod here and there as I spoke to him, and silence as I did so. And I wanted absolutely no games or magic tricks being played with forks while eating lunch. Basically I wanted him to act like an adult!

I was about to open my mouth and let loose demanding he stop doing what he was doing and look at me like a 'normal' person would, when something inside stopped me, and I realised - this isn't love!

Love is unconditional.

Love loves.

Love accepts.

And here I was clearly not loving him in this moment. I was not accepting him for who he was and I was wanting him to act in a certain way and respond a certain way. **MY** way.

This isn't love.

And it certainly isn't being open to love.

Being open to love is being open to others and their quirks. Love accepts a person, and their fork too!

I'm not saying don't discipline your children when they are out of line or are misbehaving. Because love too is discipline and most certainly corrects someone when they are wrong, disrespectful, rude, or unkind.

But my son Hugh wasn't any of those things. He wasn't being naughty, he wasn't being unkind; he hadn't done anything wrong. He was simply entertaining himself with a fork while eating lunch, which I happened to find extremely irritating!

Love doesn't make other people's choices wrong and yours right.

Love doesn't alter another person's behavior because it makes you uncomfortable.

No.

Love accepts a person for who THEY are and not who YOU wish them to be.

Love looks past those irritating little quirks and behaviors that rub us the wrong way and simply loves anyway.

As much as I wanted to yell at my son Hugh and make him stop doing what he was doing, I didn't. I let it go and decided to love him instead. And I did so by ignoring the irritating sound of the spinning fork, and when it got too much for me, I loved him by walking away and leaving the room.

And lastly, I loved him by choosing to look at it all differently and see how great he was for doing what he was doing. He was being creative, independent, and learning to entertain himself. All great skills to have in life!

Ever since I made the decision to be more open to love I realised this must include everyone, including those who have little annoying habits and quirks. And instead of closing to love when we are irritated or frustrated, choosing to love them anyway.

Because love does that.

Practice:

Next time you find yourself becoming irritated by another's behaviour, action, or little 'quirk', see if you can turn it around by letting it go and loving them instead.

    I'd love to hear how you went with this one. Please contact me and let me know. As it's one I haven't fully mastered and still challenges me.

Brave and Bold

I've said it before, but only because it's true. Being open to love is being vulnerable. It means putting yourself out there, loving others, doing kind things, and the scary possibility of having it all rejected. This is why I believe we are more likely to close to love rather than open to it.

But what if we did always open to it? Facing the possibility of being rejected and loving anyway?

I remember a day I did just that.

I opened myself up, followed my heart, and put me and my love completely out there. And as you will read, my love was 'rejected'.

But you know what?

My heart wasn't.

My heart did what it was made to do and felt good for doing so. And that my friends is all that matters.

I'll never forget it. I did something so bold, so 'out there' even for me. Yet after it all, even the rejection, I couldn't have felt more proud of myself for doing so.

I was proud because I hadn't closed myself down to love but had opened when I was really tempted not to. And I was proud because I opened right up to love in a situation I'd normally avoid and remain closed in.

It was late one afternoon, and I was on my way to pick my boys up from school. I had reversed out my driveway, and a few metres down the street, I saw her - an older lady in her mid to late 60's leaving the bus stop. I'd seen her before but never like this. Never with so many bags!

I swear, she had almost six to seven on each arm, it was crazy!

She could hardly move or walk with the amount of bags she was trying to balance. Which is probably why my attention was drawn to her in the first place.

That's when I decided.

I decided to be bold, decided to open myself right up there and then, pull over, and offer this woman a lift. A complete stranger to me.

I admit before I pulled over, I had some serious self-doubt. The voice against opening to love was very strong, telling me all the reasons not to, such as…

"Nicole don't stop, you're already running late to get the boys from school."

"And look at the inside of this car! What will she think when she gets in it?"

"And your feet, you're not even wearing shoes!"

"And who is this lady? She doesn't know you, she'll think you're weird for asking, don't do it!"

And on and on it went using everything it had against me to convince me not to pull over and love this lady.

But you know what?

I ignored it.

I ignored the voice because the kind thing to do, the right thing to do, and the most loving thing to do was pull over and offer her a lift.

So I did.

I pulled over, wound down my window, introduced myself, and asked if I could give her a lift somewhere.

She looked shocked at first like she didn't completely understand what I was saying. And I wonder if this is because, sadly in life, it isn't common for a stranger to pull over and offer someone a lift?

I explained how hard I know it can be to juggle so many heavy bags and have to walk home. And I asked her again if I could offer her a lift somewhere.

She looked at me, still shocked, almost frightened and said she didn't want any help.

Yep. She said no.

But you know what?

I wound my window up, put the car back into drive, and drove off fist pumping the air thinking how awesome what I just did was!

I was so proud of me.

She didn't say yes, and that's ok - it was her choice. But I too made a choice, and I believe I made the right one. I put myself out there, opened myself up, and faced the possibility of rejection, and survived it.

To this day, I still have no idea why she declined. Perhaps because it's not common place to accept lifts from strangers, and I can see why! Sometimes it can be dangerous.

Or perhaps it was pride and how most of us don't accept the help of others because we are so accustomed to doing everything for ourselves?

Or perhaps she thought she would 'owe' me something by accepting my help?

Whatever it was, it's ok. The choice was and will always be hers. But one thing I left her with, even if she did say no, was someone who had noticed her. Noticed her struggle and cared enough to pull over and say, "Are you ok?" and offer help. On this particular day I was a personwho did this. Who offered to love another in this way. Will it some day be you?

Practice:

Today I challenge you to put yourself out there by loving someone in a way which might make you feel a little uncomfortable and awkward. Yet you know by doing so, it will bless the person and is the right thing to do.

And if you don't see any opportunities today, then be open to the many I assure you will abound in future!

Enjoy challenging yourself with this one. The awkwardness and uncomfortable feeling you will feel is real, but I assure you the reward and growth you will experience after conquering this fear is well worth the price.

Love Isn't A Currency

Unconditional love is something I'm personally working on. Not many of us do love unconditionally. We might think we do, but we don't.

Don't get me wrong, I'm pretty sure I've nailed the unconditional love thing with my children. But when it comes to others, such as my Luke, friends, or relatives ... well there are definitely some conditions.

But I'm trying to change and remove the conditions.

In the following I share with you all about a time I caught myself being conditional in my love, and how I went about changing this conditional love to one of more openness, forgiveness, and acceptance.

As in most relationships there are always ups and downs. But on one particular day I had experienced mostly its downs.

I had spent the entire day giving. Giving my time, my love, my attention, my energy, and all I had into this person. To only in return have all this love consistently rejected and pushed away. And it hurt. Really hurt!

So what did I do?

I withdrew.

I closed myself down and held back all the love I was giving, and went on with my day. Refusing to give this person even one ounce of love from me whatsoever.

Why?

Because I wasn't getting anything back from them in return.

And that's when I realised how conditional I was being in my love. It became obvious to me I was only loving them to get something in return myself. Because if I wasn't, then I wouldn't have cared if they loved me back or not!

It was because I wasn't getting the response I desired that it had annoyed me so much, and I became upset. And if I hadn't of wanted a response it never would have bothered me how they reacted.

But it did.

Because I was being conditional!

Funny how we are as humans and how conditional we can be when we don't even realise we are being it. Because in truth, I didn't think I was being conditional at all, I was being a 'nice' person, a 'loving' person, because I was LOVING him.

But that isn't how love works, and it was a huge lesson for me.

Now every time I find myself becoming annoyed or upset by another person's response to my love, I check in with myself. I check to see if I had unintentionally added in some conditions to that love.

And if I find I have added some conditions to my love, I stop. I don't stop loving them in general, because we will always love our loved ones. But I stop loving them conditionally, in way that demands they must either love me in return or respond to my love in a way I have pre intended.

Love isn't something we trade for something in return; it's something we give because it's in us, and we can't help but give it. Love isn't currency, it is a gift!

And the more we remember this, the more open we are to gifting our love and not using it to buy love or whatever else it is we want.

Practice:

Can you think of a time you were conditional with your love?

Perhaps it was like me, and you had loved someone hoping to get something in return?

Or maybe you loved someone and quickly retracted it after they had said something you didn't like?

Think about how you could you have handled this situation differently and ask yourself if there is a way in future you could stop yourself from being so conditional in your loving?

Now challenge yourself to see if you can catch yourself being conditional in future.

Being Love - How Others Do It

"Our love must not be a thing of words and fine talk. It must be a thing of action and sincerity (1 John 3:18)."

"Life without love is death," said the great Mahatma Gandhi. I read a biography of his once and what a man he was! Prior to reading his biography I knew very little about him and knew only of his name. I'm sure we all know his name.

But why do we know it?

Because he was powerful!

What was his power?

Love. All and only ever love.

I say it so often - love **IS** powerful. It is! And Gandhi is one man who fought the world with love. And even now, 70 and more years after his death, he is still remembered and always will be.

Want to be remembered?

Then choose love.
Be love.
Your love is what will be remembered, nothing else. Just and only ever love.

Violin Love

What I love most about seeing the way others love is how much it always inspires me. And how I still find it so amazing to see how others can love someone in a way (although obvious after seeing it), I never would have thought of myself.

I love that about love.

It's always simple, always easy, always available, and there are a hundred and one ways or more to do it!

The following story is about how a woman I know loved. And what I love most about this example is she didn't love in the 'traditional' way most of us would have done in this situation. No, she took it to a whole new level! Enjoy.

A friend of mine once told me about a time she was in the city. She was by herself and walking through the main open plaza area when she heard the most beautiful piece of music being played by a violin.

She had assumed it was a cd or recording being played somewhere through speakers. However she soon realised it was a middle aged man busking.

A man she told me who although looked rather scruffy and a little disheveled, was in fact quite a good looking man for his age (which she guessed was around his late sixties or early seventies).

"I had to give him a few dollars," she told me.

"But I always give the local busking musicians a few dollars, and this guy was far better than any of them, I had to give him more," she further explained.

"But Nicole, I only had a few dollars in my purse, and although I did have a $50 note I could not give him this. It was all I had for groceries, which we really needed."

As she told me, she sounded disappointed and upset she couldn't give him more. But what she did do when she gave him the few dollars she had, I believe, far exceeded any extra money she could have given.

Because as my friend bent down to give the man the few dollars she had, she told him how great his music was, and how much she had been enjoying it moments earlier.

She went on further to tell him how she thought it was a recording playing somewhere of one of the famous violinists she knows. And before she walked away she bent down, looked the man straight in the eyes, and thanked him for the gift he had given her that day in hearing him play.

And you know what?

If that ain't love, if that ain't loving someone then I don't know what is!

I'm confident those words and all the love my friend had spoken into this man that day would have meant far more to him than any extra dollar she could have given him.

I am so proud of her and the love she gave. Proving to me although we can be 'poor', love never is. And how despite our bank balance there is always an endless supply of love.

Practice:

Can you think of a time in your own life recently where you may have loved someone but could have taken it to the next level and loved that person a little more?

Or maybe looking back now, you can see an opportunity you had to love someone easily but didn't?

Perfect! This is where it all starts.

Seeing it.

Because once you see it and recognise opportunities from your past, you are now in a position and ready to be open for the new ones yet to come. Because believe me they will!

Be on the look out today for opportunities to up the level of your love, taking it that little bit further.

Please Let Me

There is something I have noticed about how others do and be love, and that is how often they believe what they are doing or did isn't anything special at all. Because it's always something so simple and small, even common courtesy at times.

Yet what makes it so special and what makes it 'love' is the extra mile they seem to go. Or the way they do it. With so much love, determination, and such purpose. And a heart so wide open to love!

The following is about a time I saw love in a man who wasn't just doing a job – because this wasn't his job at all. But a man who saw an opportunity to love someone in such a simple way!

So simple was this gesture it is something we see every day. But I question - is it ever done the way this man did it?

With love!

With purpose!

And with no other reason than to make another person's life a little easier.

I was in a small shopping complex one day, one a little out of town and one I don't normally venture to. On my way out of the building I noticed a security guard get up from where he was and start following me.

I checked my trolley, checked my youngest son Gabe - paranoid we had unintentionally stolen something!

We hadn't. Well not that I could tell anyway.

The security guard picked up his speed and was edging closer and closer to us. Just as we were about to head out the door, he picked up his pace even more and overtook the both of us, running ahead to the door.

That's when I thought perhaps he was after someone else and not us after all.

He wasn't.

It was me he was after.

And he was now at the door

"He is blocking the exit" I thought. He wants to stop me from leaving the centre!

I was at the door now, face to face with him when he looked at me and said,

"Please let me madam."

And opened the door.

At first, I wasn't quite sure what to do, or what had happened because only moments earlier, I had created a completely different scenario in my head.

But I thanked him anyway and exited the centre, still half expecting him to follow. Because I figured if he wasn't after me or someone else, then perhaps he was also on his way out of the building.

But he just stood there and waited until I had walked through the door and closed it for me.

As I walked away I turned around to see what he would do next.

Was he still watching me?

Who was this guy?

And shouldn't he be somewhere doing security?

I watched as he turned around and walked all the way back to where he was seated previously and sit down.

I realised then the only reason he had gotten up and walked all that way, even running to overtake me and beat me to it, was to open a door for me.

What a man!

What love!

And it completely made my day.

Now anyone can open a door for someone and people open doors for me all the time, as I do for others. But never with as much determination, love, and purpose as this man.

He had gone above and beyond his duty of doing security checks and everything else his job description required of him. He had seen an opportunity to love someone and did it.

Love isn't only saying I love you or gifting someone, it's in our actions too.

And let's be honest. What other reason could there be for this man to do what he did?

Love.

That's what.

That's why.

Because what was in it for him?

Nothing. Absolutely nothing, except the satisfaction in knowing he had loved someone in whatever little way he could.

Bless those in our world who live this way daily - loving in their actions.

Practice:

Today go out of your way for someone. Surprise someone with an action of love they aren't expecting.

Example: Offering to carry someone's groceries, opening a door for someone, giving someone your parking ticket that still has credit. Seeing someone in line at the movies and surprising them with a box of popcorn for them to enjoy with the movie.

Love Is Everywhere

There are endless opportunities and only one simple rule. It must be something unexpected, unplanned and completely in the moment. Enjoy!

P.S I would love to hear all about the way you chose to do this one. If you can, please share them with me over on my facebook page - Nicole Chini Love is Everywhere - because your act will inspire so many more.

Bring Back The Wave

Being love really is simple. So simple I bet you are already doing it and not even realising what you are doing is love!
But it is.
Love is often found in simple gestures. Even in something as small as a hello, a smile, or as I'm about to share with you below, a 'wave'.
Love. It's so easy! Let's all do it more.

I was driving home when I passed a group of high school students out walking alongside the road. They appeared to be on some sort of class activity and as I passed this group of young teenagers two of the students waved at me.
So I did what I normally would do.
I waved back.
However this time something struck me. Something I don't think I've noticed or realised before.
That perhaps I am the only one who does this.
Because as soon as I had waved to these teenagers, I heard them yell out to each other, "Woo Hoo" and then become super excited I had even waved back. Their over enthusiasm and excitement made me believe perhaps they were waving to all the cars that passed that day and sadly I was the only one so far to return the gesture.
Growing up I remember my own mother being a 'waver' and doing the exact same thing I had done. She would always wave to kids waving at her from the back of a bus, or in passing cars, or alongside the road as I had done.

She would wave at random people in the street, often even initiating the wave herself. Perhaps that's where I get it from.

And when in Fiji on holiday many years ago, I noticed how all the locals would always wave and say hello to you every time you passed them. This would happen when you were driving, on a tour, or simply passing them in the street.

You didn't know them and they certainly didn't know you, yet they always welcomed you as though they did.

Yet how often do we see that here?

In our own countries?

When did we all become so closed and unopened to love and friendliness?

Bring back the wave. Bring back open hearts, bring back the smiles and hellos to complete strangers.

Bring back love.

And you can bring it all back by simply saying hello, waving or both.

Practice:

Yep, you guessed it. Today's practice is to wave at someone, preferably someone you don't know. Now I get it, this one is challenging. Because if you don't know this person, what will they think?

Who cares!

Let them think what they like and just love them anyway.

So easy! Super fun and I know you can do it. Enjoy

She Loves Her Husband

I know a lady who does love in one of the most simplest ways possible. And just wait until you hear what it is!

Perhaps you have done this for someone you love?

Or maybe you know someone who does?

When this lady told me what she did, I was surprised because it was the first time I had ever heard of a wife doing it for her husband, as usually, it's a parent to their child.

And because it was a wife to her husband, not an adult to child, or done out of obligation or a need, is what truly made this act nothing but love.

When she first told me, I assumed he had problems with his eyesight and embarrassingly I asked if he did. He didn't.

"No he can read perfectly well," she told me.

"It's something I have always done for him, for us both."

What is this something she does for him every night and the special moment they both share?

She reads to him - her husband.

He in his recliner, her sitting in her own chair right beside him. With a cup of tea in one hand, book in the other.

Why?

Because as she tells me, "He loves it when I read to him." They have been doing it for years, since they married in fact.

Isn't that just the sweetest!

And it had me questioning my own intimate relationships. Whether I would be so kind, thoughtful, and so willing to do something for someone just because they like it, regardless of whether I wanted to or liked it as well?

I'd like to say I would, but the truth is I probably wouldn't. Not unless I too was getting something out of it.

This lady I know however does get something out of reading to her husband every single night. The knowledge in knowing by doing so, her husband is being loved.

Practice:

Today can you do something for someone you love? Something they enjoy which you may not?

Personally I cannot begin to tell you how many times I've played hide and go seek with my sons. Although I enjoyed this game as a child, let me tell you, as a fully grown adult, hiding in small places such as in cupboards or behind couches is not so fun.

Yet I still did it.

Why?

Because my sons enjoyed it.

Other examples may include letting someone else choose what you watch on TV or the movie you see. Knowing it may not be your first choice, but it's theirs so you go with it.

Loving others is often doing things they enjoy versus what you enjoy. Because love gives, it never takes. Give to another today. Making their choice yours. Enjoy.

He Sent Me A Text

Do you want to know how to love others?

Watch children. They do it all the time.

And most of the time they do it without words, using instead sweet little open hearted gestures.

The following example and story I want to share with you, is about a time love was expressed with words from a child.

Yet it wasn't so much the words that were said but how these words were expressed, that made this act of love so pure and one I haven't forgotten since. Enjoy.

I was cooking dinner in the kitchen when I heard my phone beep; it was a text message. I looked at my phone and noticed it was from my Luke, which I found strange as he was only in the room next to me on the couch watching tv. I opened it anyway and went on to read what it said. It said only three words,

"Hugh. Loves. You."

I looked to where Luke was seated, and it was obvious he did not send the message. No phone was in sight, and he was caught up with something else. I knew then that it must have been Hugh (which up until this point, I had no idea he even knew what a text message was or how to send one, considering Hugh wasn't even of school age yet and barely five).

I went to find Hugh and saw him playing games on Luke's phone. Hugh looked up at me casually and said, "Hey mum, did you get the message?"

"I sure did buddy," I said to him as I wrapped him up in one gigantic big mum cuddle.

And it wasn't all I did because, immediately after receiving the text I had sent one straight back to him saying, "Mum loves him more."

That was almost nine years ago now and I've never forgotten it, and never will forget it.

Why?

Because it reminds me how simple it really is to love someone.

Yes, sure, anyone can send a text, and we do it all the time. But do you do it the way my fiveyear old son had? For no other reason than to brighten another's day and remind them they are loved?

Hugh didn't have to do this. He could have sat with Luke's phone and played games like most young boys his age would want to do the moment they score a parent's phone - but he didn't.

Well he did.

But not before putting his own five year old desires aside for a moment to tell his mum how much he loves her by surprising her in the kitchen with a text message.

And if that aint love in action, then what is?

Practice:

Today see if you can place a message of love somewhere you know the person you are wanting to love will find it.

Examples are writing a note and slipping it into their bag, laptop or computer. Sticking it on the steering wheel of the car or a fridge. Leaving it next to the toaster, their toothbrush or even inside their favourite cereal box you know they'll reach into in the morning.

The main element here is surprise. And planning ahead! Enjoy this one.

She Feeds Birds

We are all beautiful, us humans. Each of us all having our own unique way to love.

And I find it so incredibly amazing how love can come in so many different forms and be done in so many different ways.

One of my desires for this book is by reading all the different ways love is; you too will begin to see and notice the love in your own life and in the lives of others.

The following is about a time recently I saw love in the life of a little old lady. A lady who shared with me something she did. Something, which to her was not love, just something she did.

But that's not the way I saw it.

I saw love.

I saw her being love in a way unique to her. In a way she enjoyed. In a way only she could.

One of my jobs was working in supermarkets promoting all sorts of products, and I absolutely loved it!

Why?

You'd think it would be all the free samples I scored, or the fabulous hours and being my own boss. But honestly, what I love most about it is the people I meet and the stories they share.

So many stories, some heartwarming, some heartbreaking, all beautiful. But there is one sweet lady I remember most of all.

She was old, very old. And I saw her in the pet food aisle struggling with the most oversized bag of bird seed I think I had ever seen. I'm talking a five kilo bag or more. Naturally I ran to help and couldn't help but ask her,

"Do you have birds at home?"

"No dear," she replied.

Now I was even more curious.

Please tell me she isn't eating it, I thought to myself as I know how many on a pension can struggle.

"I feed the wild birds that come into our yard during the winter months looking for food," she explained.

"I have no pets and I live alone dear," she continued.

"The birds bring me so much joy, and no matter what happens every month, I always make sure I've enough money saved to purchase a big bag of wild bird seed."

I had no words. I stood there looking at this sweet old lady feeling as though my heart had been ripped right open.

I wanted to buy the bag of birdseed for her, I wanted to buy an entire years supply of birdseed for this woman. But I didn't.

It didn't feel right to do or offer such a thing, because buying the seed was her thing. Not mine. Hers. The way she loves, the way she gives back a little to the beautiful world we all live in. So I did the very next best thing.

I simply smiled, hugged her, and said,

"Thank you."

"Oh my sweet dear," she replied, "the birds give me so much more than I could ever give them."

Perhaps she was right.

But what she didn't know was that day, she gave me far more than I ever could have given her.

She inspired me. She opened my heart. And she reminded me how easy it is to love.

With so little, this lady gave so much.

She gave the love in her heart to the native birds that call her place home.

Practice:

Do you have a unique way you love others, someone, or something? Is there something you enjoy and do that others may not?

I have a friend who loves to knit. She's never had children herself, and therefore, no grandchildren. But she knits beanies, booties, and blankets for those who do. It is her unique way to give by doing something she loves.

We all have our own personal interests and likes. Could you possibly use one of yours to gift another?

The Little Girl Who Gifted Me

The following is a story about a time when I saw a little girl love. She loved me. And in a way only a five year old could.

I loved her too that day.

I loved her by accepting and receiving her love and not refusing it. Which, at times, we so often do. Even if unintentionally!

Because the way others love you may not always be the way you would love or even the way you would like to be loved. But love is love in all its various forms. And to give love it needs to be received.

In the following story I share how, for one little girl to love me fully, I had to receive it and let her give me love.

I was working one night in a job I had which I absolutely loved. I worked in a social club doing bar work. However, most of my shifts were up in the club's restaurant. I loved these shifts most as they offered a lot more interaction with members as they dined on their meal.

One night in particular, I was clearing glasses when a little girl seated at the table started chatting to me excitingly. She told me all about her new shoes, her new dress, and her absolute new favourite, two big shiny, sparkling dress rings which she wore proudly, one on each hand.

I told her how much I loved her rings and how beautiful she looked in all her new things.

Later during my shift, this same little girl called me back over to her table and begun pulling off one of her rings. It came off easy, as the ring was a bit big for her. She then placed the ring she had removed from her hand into my hands, looked up at me, and said,

"This is for you. It's my favorite one, but I want you to have it. I know you will take good care of it for me and will love it as much as I do."

It took a lot for me not to break down and cry at the generosity and love I was just given from this little girl.

If she had been an adult I probably wouldn't have accepted it. I would have refused, stating reasons why I couldn't take it. But this little girl was looking up at me with so much happiness in her eyes, such love, and so much joy; I knew if I didn't accept her gift, it would crush her.

She wanted to gift me.

She wanted to love me.

And love me the only way she could. With a gift of her own!

And I accepted it.

Accepted it because had I not, then this wouldn't be loving her.

And as hard as it was for me to take the ring on that night, I had to. Not for me, but for her. For love. For her to know her love wasn't a mistake, wasn't refused, wasn't handed back. But was accepted with an open heart as wide as hers.

I still have the ring. I don't wear it and to be honest, don't think I have since the night she gave it to me. But I have kept it as a reminder to love more - as a reminder of the joy in giving someone something of which has great value to you.

Children. They really do know how to love.

What a beautiful place the world would be if we all loved a little more like them.

Practice:

Is there something you own which you value? Something, which you could gift to another? Perhaps something, which was once dear to you and isn't anymore, and for whatever reason, you still hold onto it?

Or maybe a friend recently commented on a fabulous pair of earrings or a new handbag you own, saying how much they loved it. Would you be willing to part with this? As an act of love?

This practice can be challenging as we hold so tightly onto things we own and love. But like the little girl in the story I shared, giving such a gift is an act of love that will never ever be forgotten.

Dancing With The Fat Girl

I love how you always remember love. You may forget all the other details which happened at the time, but you never forget the love. Love always stands out, is always felt, and is mostly the only detail ever remembered.

In the following story I share about a time I was loved, I do remember the details, well one in particular - the song playing at the time. Because now every time I hear this song all I remember is the love I felt and was given by a 13-year-old boy.

To him it wasn't love, just kindness. But love and kindness, it's all the same thing. It's all love when you act from your heart and not your head.

Driving to pick my boys up from school, I heard the song 'End of the Road' by Boys II Men come on the radio. And I was taken back - taken back to a time when I was 13.

It was my first year in high school and my first high school dance. And there was a boy, a boy named Ben, who slow danced with me. He was the only boy with the heart to say yes to the 'fat girl'. And he was the first boy I had ever danced with, the only boy, throughout all of my years of high school to say yes.

I have never forgotten it and never will.

Because every time I hear the song 'End of Road' by Boys II Men on the radio, I always think of Ben. The only boy in a school full of them to say yes and make me feel loved. A boy who for a moment let go of his own self-image and reputation, not caring what others thought to dance with me, the fat girl.

Thank you Ben. I never thanked you. I danced, I smiled, I felt loved and when you walked away I was secretly in love with you for the rest of the year. Today I'm sure you've forgotten about it, but I haven't. And right here, right now, in this book in a chapter all about how others love, I want to thank you. Thank you for loving me that day.

And I thank you for showing me, and all those who read this how love works. How love ignores stereotypes, peer pressures, and ridicule, and loves, regardless. No matter your size. No matter your status. No matter what. It just loves. Always. Dancing with the girl no one else would.

Practice:

Is there someone from your past who did a kind and loving act towards you? An act of love so kind you've never forgotten?

Thank them today.

Write them a letter, call them, or send them a text to say thank you. And if you are no longer in contact with this person or have no way of contacting them, then thank them in your heart today. Thanking them for the beautiful way they loved you way back.

Love Forgives

Some people do love so effortlessly. Like children.

For me, some days, being love can seem anything but natural, where for others it's no effort at all, just a way of life.

And that is exactly the way I want to live. Effortlessly loving always.

The following is about a time when I witnessed my young sons doing exactly that - loving effortlessly by being love in one of the most essential, yet often hardest ways we can ever love. Through forgiveness!

It was the last week of the holidays and my boys had finally hit the point they seem to do every school holiday break - over it. Or more so over each other!

In particular, it was Hugh, the eldest, who had lost it the most. And Julian being the younger brother, bore the brunt of it. There was yelling, there were tears, a brotherly punch or two. You get the idea, it was messy.

Yet twenty minutes later I caught them both back together in the same room laughing, and acting as though nothing had happened. Wow! I thought. If it was me, I'd be thinking about what happened and holding onto the injustice and anger of it all!

But not my Julian!

Nor Hugh!

Because everything that had occurred twenty minutes earlier was now utterly and completely forgotten about and in the past. They had both moved on. Both been forgiven, and both received the other's forgiveness.

I wondered in that moment, if I could ever forgive someone as quickly as Julian had forgiven his brother Hugh? And I wondered if I could receive as easily as Hugh had the forgiveness his brother gave. I'm not sure I could have.

However Julian and his brother both did!

And you know how they did this?

By being love and displaying something many of us have forgotten, what true forgiveness is and looks like.

Love! That's what.

Because love forgives.

And love will always forgive someone for a moment of insanity, knowing this moment of insanity isn't who they are, and who they are is what love is forgiving. Not the action. Not the insanity. But for them. The person they have always been and the person they have always loved.

Julian didn't forgive his brother's punch, mean words, and actions; he forgave his brother. The brother he loves, the brother he has always loved, and the brother who loves him, not his actions.

We can learn so much from children.

Practice:

Can you forgive someone today?

Can you find it in your heart to forgive someone whose actions towards you may have been unloving and unkind?

An action, which you didn't deserve, and one which may have caused you a lot of pain.

Can you forgive them? Not the action or what they did, but the person who did it.

Forgive today. Forgive always! It will bring you so much love, freedom and joy when you release the pain once held in your heart.

Being Love Is Simple

"If there is anything better than being loved, it's doing the loving."

Love is always simple. It always was.
Only we complicated it.
You don't need a reason to love - you don't even need another person to love. All you need is a heart so open to love, all it can do is love.

There was a time in my life when I thought the only way to experience love was to have someone to love. Or have someone love me. I have since learned that this is in fact not true. You don't need anyone! You just need you. And your love!

Why wait for someone to love? Or for someone to love you?

When love is available right here and right now.

Love is something that comes from within you. It lives in you. And is there right now even as you read these words. How great is that!

You don't need a person, reason, or excuse to love. You just be it, be love. And that is truly the most awesome thing about love.

In the following pages, I share with you ways others and I have loved in the most simplest way, and just how easy it is to do this very thing we all call love.

Enjoy!

Sitting on The Bus

How does someone 'be' love?

What is 'being love' anyway and why is it so simple?

Because it is.

Not the best answer I know. But honestly, being love really is simple!

The only reason we think it isn't is because we have made up ideas as to what love is and how it should look. When the truth is love doesn't really look like anything. Love isn't a 'look' or something to be 'seen', but felt!

So if you are feeling love, you're being love. And if you can feel the feeling of love, of kindness, of compassion, and all those other wonderful things that love makes us feel, then quite frankly, you are being loved.

The following is about a time when I was being love by really doing nothing at all. In fact I didn't even have to move a muscle to do it. It was that simple.

And right now, I guarantee you can do it too. All you need is yourself, some love, and someone to send it to.

Try it. And get back to me.

I remember sitting on a bus going to Sydney once. I was off on a weekend away just for me. It was a three-hour long journey, so I sat back, relaxed, and was enjoying the quiet time away from 'being a mummy'. After a few minutes of this I was bored.

I had books, I'd read a few pages, but I was still bored and wanting something more. I soon realised what I was wanting was to 'do' something not just sit there. So I began looking around the bus for something to do when I spotted him, the bus driver.

I could see his face in the reflection of the revision mirror above his head. And that's when it came to me. A thought,

'I could love this man, And I could right now in this very moment bless him.'

So I did!

How?

Easy.

I sent him love.

Love is simple. It really is. And is honestly as simple as sending someone love. So as I sat on this bus ride from my hometown to another, I decided to send love to a man I did not know - the bus driver.

How this looks exactly is different for everyone. And to be honest, to look at it you are not really seeing anything at all, just me sitting on a bus and the man I was blessing driving it.

But what is happening on the inside of me is what matters most and makes all the difference.

Because as I was sitting there on the bus, I was silently and intentionally filling up my own heart with as much love as I possibly could. And then once it was as full as I could get it, I sent it to this man.

I did so by imagining the love I had built up leaving me and entering this man's heart. I was basically projectile shooting this man love bullets!

He had no idea.

And that's what I love so much about doing this sort of thing. This man (the bus driver) had no idea that as he drove down the long strip of narrow highway, there was a complete stranger a few seats behind him, blessing him, loving him. And although he wasn't aware of this, I'm certain on some level he felt it.

I've done this before. It isn't new to me. It's something I started a while ago when I first walked down this 'being love' path. And honestly it's life-changing. Because not only does it make you feel good it opens your heart to others.

And think about it for a moment.

What if it were you? What if you were the man driving the bus that day?

Wouldn't you want someone praying over you and blessing you with love as you drove?

I know I would!

So why not, on your next long trip with nothing better to do, spend a few minutes sending a stranger love?

In fact why not everywhere!

In the grocery line…

In traffic…

Whilst sitting across from someone at dinner.

Any time everywhere; love is in you waiting to be used. Waiting to be sent.

Love really is that simple.

Practice:

Like in the story above, love blast someone today without telling them, or them knowing you are doing it!

It will take a minute or less of your time, can be done anywhere, at anytime. And the most amazing part is, it can even be done to someone who isn't physically nearby.

Yep. You can send love right now to your dear friend who lives miles away, or your grandma who isn't feeling well, or to someone abroad you heard is suffering and needs love.

There is absolutely no excuse not to do this one. And of all the practices throughout this book, this is by far the easiest and most simplest to do. Enjoy.

Loving By Seeing

You know what feels damn good?
Being loved!
Especially when it's by people you hardly know and people who aren't even all that close to you. People you wouldn't normally expect to love you. People, who were not brought up loving you, like your family, friends, parents, or your children.
I'm talking about people who haven't known you all too long, people who may have only just come into your life, and even people who are complete strangers. That kind of love - and man does it feel good!
I remember once being loved in a simple way by people I hardly knew, and even to this day I am still loved by others this way.
It's such a simple and beautiful way to love, which is exactly why I want to share it here. To remind us all how easy love really is to do.

I was walking into work to start my shift for the evening when I passed some regular customers seated at a table. As soon as I passed them, I overheard them say to each other with excitement and joy,
"Oh there she is! We missed her."
I'd been gone a week. If that!
Yet these three words, three single words said with such enthusiasm, excitement, sincerity and love, filled me up like nothing else.
"We missed her," or more commonly "We missed you," when said so genuinely and authentically straight from the heart is love. And those regular customers that night practiced it so perfectly – by simply expressing it!

They expressed what they were feeling in the moment with full feeling, honesty, and love to the person they were feeling it towards. Me!

It always feels so good to be appreciated, seen, and recognized for what you do. And it is why, when in shopping centres, I make a conscious effort to smile, make eye contact with and wholeheartedly thank those who serve me with such great customer service. And on good days when I'm completely walking the 'love walk', I even bless those who don't give me the best service!

I've made it a habit to make eye contact with people and smile and connect with others I don't know. Even people, who haven't 'served' me in some way, people who pass me by or people I see seated in a cafe, or waiting in line at a store.

Why?

So they feel seen and loved.

To see another is to love them - to appreciate someone is to love them. To smile at someone, make eye contact with or say hello, is loving someone. It really is that simple but how often do we do it?

How often do we really 'see' another person?

See them for who they are, what they do or appreciate them? Because it honestly is one of the simplest ways to love someone.

And being on the receiving end of this kind of love a few times myself, I can tell you not only does it feel damn good; it makes you feel loved. So loved.

Practice:

Love someone in person today by using words.

You could tell one of your family members you love them. You know you do - they know you do. But when was the last time you actually told them with words?

Or you could sincerely thank the next person who helps you. Or how about going out of your way to say hello to someone you don't know? Ask them how their day has been or wishing them a great one!

So many options!

But remember it is vital eye contact be made when doing this and your full attention be one hundred percent on them.

Why?

Because this is what makes it more powerful and more sincere, than if you only half-heartedly do it or your attention is elsewhere.

Have fun being love with words. It's one of my personal favourite ways to use love.

Post It Sandwiches

Love isn't limited. It's Vast!

Love isn't one way. It's all ways!

And love most certainly isn't always done the same way or even in the way we think it needs to be.

Love can be creative.

In fact love NEEDS to be creative. Because the person you are loving is unique, and every situation will be different. And if you love someone the same way every time - well let's be honest, it gets kinda stale.

So spice things up, mix up your love, get a little creative with it, but mostly keep it simple - because love is always simple.

In the following, I share one way I went a little creative with love, while keeping it so incredibly simple! You must try this one. It's easy. Simple. And so much fun!

Post it notes! I love them!

Do you know those little bright yellow square note pads that often come in a variety of colours? The ones with a sticky edge at the top designed for you to stick somewhere. Yep, those. I absolutely love those things and they are a total must have for me.

Why?

Because I use them as weapons of love!

I'm a note sticker, and I've committed so many love bombs with these things, it could almost be criminal. I'm talking in toilet cubicles, stuck to bills I've paid, inside cards and letters to people, anywhere and everywhere I can add some love with words on a post it. I've done it.

But one of my absolute favourites, is the love note bombs I do for my children. I love it. And I always do it in advance, preparing them the night before, so they don't know it's there until they see it.

Where do I put this little post it note of love?

In their lunchbox stuck to the top of their sandwiches.

It all started with a simple "I love you" or a "Don't forget mums love you" and, a "Have

a nice day" but has since developed into more phrases of love.

Now I wish I could take credit here saying I totally came up with this great idea myself, but the truth is, I didn't. I remember my mum doing it and sticking a little piece of paper (this was pre-post it days) inside my lunch saying, she loved me.

I was in high school (and yep, my mother still made my lunch in high school!) but you know what? Although a teenager, I wasn't embarrassed by this or her notes. I loved it!

In fact I started to look forward to them and on the days there wasn't one, I really missed it.

It is only later now as an adult I've thought more about it. I thought about how she would take the time every night after a long day at work to write me a little note. She didn't have to. But she did. Why? One reason only -

Love.

To love me!

And in one of the most simplest ways possible – she told me. But as we all know, they are only words. But words, when written and stuck somewhere purposely with one agenda only – to love you, is so powerful and so much more than only words. And I assure you it will be something you never forget.

Practice:

Although love is an everyday thing, sometimes we need to branch out a little and get creative - blasting our loved ones with a surprise love bomb or two stuck to sandwiches.

How can you be creative with your love today? Maybe like I had done you may wish to write some posts of love and sneak them in places your loved ones will find. Or you may want to be a little more 'out there' with your creative love and write I love you on the mirror with lipstick, or spell it out in stones on the sidewalk?

Or maybe you're feeling super duper completely inspired and creative and wish to write a song, poem, paint a picture, or colour in and gift this to another with love.

The choice is yours and you are only limited by your imagination.

I Was All Ears

Did you know that sometimes to love someone you don't really have to do anything at all?

I'm serious.

Sometimes loving someone is simply standing there listening. Or being with someone as they cry, and handing them a tissue.

Love isn't always an action that requires a lot from us; sometimes it requires very little. Such as listening and offering yourself as someone to talk to about their problems. And in the following, I share with you how I did exactly that - loved someone simply by listening.

Love is simple it's only us who believe it's difficult.

I'm a listener. Probably because I dislike talking about myself. So when it comes to conversations with others, I'm usually the one doing the listening.

And I love it.

At work, I'm most guilty of this. I am surprised I haven't lost a job because of it! You see, I am always with customers, clients, and complete strangers for far too long doing what appears to be just standing there chatting. When really, I'm not. I'm listening.

And believe me it's a kindness. And it's love.

So many people in this world want to be heard and listened to. Yet sadly, not many get the opportunity.

I remember one night while working, I stood and listened to a couple tell me with tears in their eyes, of the pain they were both currently going through. They didn't want me to fix it, feel sorry for them, or even help. They simply wanted me to listen.

So listen I did. I was all ears.

We all have ears. And we can offer them every day as a way to love others simply by listening. And what a beautiful kindness this is!

There is a reason we were born with one mouth and two ears. More listening, less talking! Well that's what I believe anyway.

So if you're ever in a situation where you don't know how to love someone or what to do, try loving them by listening. By being still and doing nothing. Just hearing what needs to be said and what they have to say. Because believe me listening, more often than not, is exactly what they want and need.

And it's love.

Practice:

Next time someone talks to you or begins a conversation, listen to them. Don't offer advice or talk about how your own life is going, just simply listen to their story. I challenge you to see how long you can do this without speaking up and giving in to the urge to talk.

Now I warn you here, this one is challenging! Because you will find the urge to reply will be strong. But I know you can do it!

The main thing to remember is unless they ask you a question directly, remain silent. You'll be amazed at what will be revealed and how much deeper the conversation will become. And I can guarantee that this mere act of simply 'just listening' is one of the biggest kindnesses of love you could ever offer to the person talking to you. Enjoy.

Bringing Light (and Wind!)

Being love is sometimes as easy as having a conversation with someone and helping them move closer to love by sharing a different perspective.

This is one way I live love often, so often it's become a habit of mine I don't even realise I'm doing. Some people may call it 'being positive', and people have even called me this. However, I don't feel it is. I feel it's much deeper than just 'being positive'.

Because honestly sometimes in life, a situation will arise that no matter how you look at it, it will never be positive. However, there is always love and no matter how positive or negative a situation may be, love never leaves you. It may just be it is hidden and wrapped up in another perspective requiring you to view the whole situation differently.

The following is an example of this, me viewing a situation differently than someone who also experienced the same situation except without love.

I experienced it with love, gratitude and was blessed by it. This person viewed it as something negative, which caused her to feel angry, annoyed, and fearful, and all those other not so nice feelings.

The choice to choose love is always ours. And one way we can choose love and bless another is by simply looking for it and then sharing it. Especially when the other person cannot see it for themselves.

We experienced some incredible winds one day. So incredible that everyone was talking about it. And whilst at work the following day a lady I did not know, struck up a conversation about it. She complained the entire time, going on and on about how crazy the wind was, how it had kept her awake all night, and how horrible her night was because of it all - until I said,

"You know what I was thinking last night as I heard the crazy wind bashing against the house and windows?" (I didn't give her a chance to respond and continued),

"I kept thinking how blessed and lucky I was to be inside with a roof over my head, warm and not outside.

"And I kept thinking about all those who weren't so lucky, those who weren't protected from it. Like animals and pets that live outside and, of course, the homeless."

And she stood there. Silent for a moment then said,

"Yeah. I never thought of it that way."

And that's when I realised I had just committed a great act of kindness and an even bigger act of love.

I had sown a little love into this woman.

Not intentionally, but I had for a moment done it. I had changed this woman from feeling victimized, negative and 'against the world' to being grateful.

Sowing love into the world and being love is what I often refer to as bringing light. Where you shine onto to others, love, in whatever way you can by uplifting them as you go about your day. On a good day, this is what I do. I help remind those of us in the world who have forgotten how blessed we are.

And love sometimes is simply just that, reminding.

Reminding others of all the wonderful things that we are blessed with but simply forget.

Practice:

For the next 24 hours, look for situations that you can completely turn around and choose to see in a whole new way. Perhaps something didn't go as planned, or something was cancelled, your favourite store was closed, or you ruined the cake you spent the day baking.

Is there a way you can turn this situation into a better one?

Can you see this in a different way?

Maybe the ruined cake gave your more patience and practice to improve the next one? Or it allowed you to use your creativity and turn ruined cake into a trifle or cake balls.

Or your favourite store being closed allowed you to finally venture into the new one around the corner.

And possibly, the plans/date being cancelled freed up your time, which you then spent doing something even more amazing!

Whatever happens, be on the look out for the next 24 hours for the blessing in disguise, the light in the darkness. Because I assure you, any and all situations can be turned by a slight change in perspective.

The Girl Who Sang

One way to 'be love' is by appreciating others. Yet how often do we do this?

We may appreciate others and what they do, did, or are doing for us, but do we express it?

Do we put our love into action by appreciation?

There are many ways you can appreciate someone, through words, gifts, gestures, hugs. But my absolutely favourite - telling them!

It's my favourite because I am someone who loves to be appreciated by words. To be thanked in person always leaves me feeling so much more love than had the person not appreciated me with words, and I had only assumed they did.

In life we often assume the other person knows they are appreciated. But do they? And if they do, would it hurt telling them again?

Never!

It would only make them feel even more loved!

In the following I share with you all about a time I appreciated someone - simply by telling them. I could have kept this appreciation and love to myself, but I didn't. I shared it, and I told her, even though she was a complete stranger.

I was on a bus, after a big day out and I was seated behind a young girl when all of a sudden she began singing in another language. It was so beautiful. So I told her.

At first I didn't want to. I thought it would embarrass her, or truthfully, it was me who was embarrassed to say something.

But I told her anyway.

I told her because we all need to be encouraged in life.

I told her because I loved her voice and the freedom this young girl sang with, having not a care in the world.

I told her because we all love how good it feels when another person acknowledges us.

And I told her because I had to.

I had to because in a few year's time, she may never do this. She will be older and perhaps too self-conscious and reluctant to sing in public. She may doubt herself and care far too much about what others think. When they are probably thinking exactly the same thing I was that day, how beautiful her voice is.

So that's why I told her.

I told her with the hope my words will be something she remembers, when for whatever reason in future, she feels she can no longer sing so freely and openly in public.

And if that ever were to happen, I hope she looks back and remembers me. Remembers a lady on a bus once who heard her singing and told her how wonderful and truly beautiful her voice was and is, and the gift she has to give.

And I hope and pray this dear sweet little girl has never stopped singing and continues to gift her gift. And I hope and pray she always, always, remembers just how beautiful, loved, and appreciated her voice was and always will be.

Practice:

Today find one person you can appreciate and tell them. Or if you cannot tell them in person send a text message, letter, or call them to tell them, thank you and you appreciate them.

The list of people you can appreciate today is endless. Your children, your parents, your neighbor, a co-worker, store attendant, your favourite artist, or even the postman!

Just a simple, "Hi Simon, thank you so much for opening the door for me, driving me to work, passing on the message, looking out for me, delivering my mail etc. etc. - I appreciate you."

I'd love to hear how you went with this one. If you feel called please reach out and contact me or visit my facebook page and group.

I Said Thank You

The ultimate in being love is when it becomes a part of who you are. You walk, breathe and live love. Where everything you do is done in love. It's possible, it really is! And to be honest, it's probably simpler than you think.

Because love isn't always the grand gestures we think it is. Nor is it something which requires a lot of effort or masses of time. Yeah, sure, it can be, but most the time it simply does not.

Being love can be practiced every day in something as simple as a thank you. Not just a quick thank you as someone passes you a plate or opens the door for you - although this too is wonderful and a huge must in situations like it.

But I'm talking more here about saying thank you when it isn't expected, or saying thank you when it requires effort on your part, now that is love.

Saying thank you is always being love. I get it. But when said with motive, purpose, and done when it's not required or expected, and simply because you want to, powerful. And it's one of the most beautiful and sincere ways a thank you can be expressed.

The following is about a time I expressed a thank you in such a way.

I heard a really beautiful song on the radio. It was a song I hadn't heard before and it had the most amazing lyrics. I absolutely loved it. So do you know what I did?

I contacted the radio station.

Yep. I actually did that.

I contacted them just to say how much I had loved the song they had played and to thank them for playing it.

I do this often (not contact radio stations, though perhaps I could do this one more often), but thank people.

I've always been thankful and grateful, but I usually leave it at that. Never saying anything more, just feeling it and keeping it all to myself. And I most certainly never thank people when it requires some effort, like calling someone or contacting a radio station! Especially if it means going out of my way to do so!

It's only since walking the love path that I began to take it a lot more seriously and really get into it and express my gratitude and love. And you know what?

People absolutely love it!

I have written thank you notes to the library, to teachers, to department stores, and even my postman has received a thank you from me.

Basically everyone who has really touched or helped me in some way, I thank. It's such a simple thing to do - to thank someone.

But how often do we do it?

I admit before my love walk, I never did. I always assumed people knew and didn't need thanking. Now I thank others almost daily.

Why?

Because people want to be appreciated and thanked. They may not say it but they do, and when they are they feel loved.

Love is simple. It really is. So simple it can be done using only two words. Thank you.

Practice:

Today as you go about your day, see how many opportunities arise to say thank you. And do it - say thank you. It could be to a person, a situation, or even something as crazy as a radio station like I did in the story above.

One thing is for sure, I guarantee, is there will be endless opportunities to say thank you. It could even be saying thank you to yourself for the time you have made right now to read this book. Or thank you to the person who gave you the book, or to yourself for buying it.

Or maybe you're sitting inside warm, thanks to your heating, or cool thanks to the air conditioning. Who set this up for you? Who pays the bills? Who do you have to thank for such things?

I challenge you to find at least one person today to say thank you to and appreciate. Even if the only person you thank and appreciate is yourself. Because it matters, it all matters. And it's all love.

Favourites

I want to share something I've been doing with my kids for many years now. It's a bedtime ritual we call 'favorites'. And I want to share it because it is such a simple way to love. And isn't only restricted to children either!

Because honestly, you can use this on absolutely anybody and believe me they will love it!

Let me explain more…

My children when growing up, like most children, would always want a bedtime story and to be 'tucked' in at night. Which I happily had always done and really enjoyed, for my first son, however by the time my second and eventually third son came around, I was well and truly over it!

That sounds awful doesn't it?

Truthfully though I kind of was over it.

I wasn't over them or saying goodnight, just really bored with the same old routine and books I'd read so many times before. I wanted more. And I knew this special time at night just before my boys drift off to sleep could be something more.

And then one night it struck me.

An idea, which little did I know at the time, would change everything in our home and our bedtime routines forever.

As I write this book my eldest son is now a teenager and still asks for 'favourites'. He doesn't ask for a book to be read or to be tucked in, because let's face it, most children as they approach or are in their teenage years stop requesting the bedtime story and to be tucked in! But 'favourites'… now that is another story! Because I guarantee they will never stop asking for these.

What are favourites?

'Favourites' are every night when putting your children to bed you share with them a favourite thing about your day. And then you ask them for theirs.

For me when I first started doing 'favourites' I would always choose something my boys had done that day which I loved, and would share with them how much what they did had helped me or made me proud. Or other times I would share my own 'favourite' like the sun shining after so many days of rain.

I remember how it had all started.

One night my boys had watched something on television, which had frightened them, and I remember how worried I was about them having bad dreams. And to be more honest, more concerned about getting up in the middle of the night to deal with it! So I wanted to send them off to sleep with happy thoughts.

But how could I do this?

That's it I thought! I could fill them up with happy thoughts.

So I began sharing with them all the happy things that had happened during the day. It was such a success, the very next night, we did it again. And the night after that and the night after that, until eventually it started to develop into something more.

No longer was it about giving them 'happy' thoughts so they sleep well (which naturally happens anyway when you end your day and fall to sleep with happy thoughts), but it was now a way we could share and express gratitude and love about our day.

My boys absolutely loved hearing 'favourites' every night and I found myself consciously looking throughout the day for what would be the night's 'favourite'. It was usually something we had done together or a kind action I had witnessed them doing. These were their 'favourites' to hear. They would always love hearing about how proud they had made me, or how much I had loved something they had done.

It's praise at its best!

As my sons have become older I'm seeing less of them now. My eldest is in high school so a 'my favourite is when you used your manners and said thank you to your brother' doesn't quite cut it anymore. So naturally it's adjusted and grown with them.

Now as I tuck them in to bed at night I ask them what their favourite thing was during their day. It usually varies from 'playing with my friend Josh at lunch' to 'our maths teacher was away so I had a really easy class and the maths quiz was cancelled'.

Sometimes it's a 'nothing'. 'Nothing was my favourite' my boys will tell me. In which case I accept it as their answer and share my favourite with them. It will usually be two things. The first gratitude and love for them in some way. Such as them coming home from school safely, giving me a cuddle, putting the dishes in the sink, or how quickly they had dressed for school.

It can be anything really.

The second is always a favourite from my day. Such as the peace I felt after a stressful day, the shops having our favourite brand of ice-cream on sale, or meeting up with a friend. It's never the same. Always different! And you know what - I'm not bored of it yet. Not even after almost eight years of doing this. It never gets stale, never grows old, and I find myself actually looking forward to our 'favourites' every night before bed.

I absolutely love we do this, and I can honestly say it is one of the best things I have ever incorporated (even if by accident) into our family. It is something that has changed all of our lives for the better and only strengthened our relationship with each other.

And I'm confident in saying, by doing this simple little act of 'favorites' yourself, your life too will change, and every relationship you have in it. Because 'favourites' is a way of sharing love in one of the simplest and easiest ways possible.

It takes less than five minutes and the impact it has is beyond anything you or I could ever imagine. So why not give it a go and ask yourself now,

What was my favourite thing today?

And then when you think of it, go share it with someone and ask them theirs. See what happens. You may just be surprised.

Practice:

Tonight before bed share with a loved one a favourite thing about your day. Or if you haven't a loved one to share with then simply write it down and share it with yourself. I challenge you to do this every night for a week!

Return Or Complain

Being love is a daily act where in everyday situations you look for ways to add a little love. The following is another example of how easily we can love simply by saying thank you and giving praise.

However this example goes a little further.

It's about a time when I was so determined to say thank you and send love, I didn't allow it not being possible, to let it not be possible!

And I hope by sharing this, it inspires you to never give up on giving love even when it appears hard to do so, doesn't seem possible, or something is blocking you! Because as you will see with love, there is always a way.

It may not be the traditional way or a way you're familiar with, but there will always be a way. And love will find it!

So let it.

All companies and businesses have them. Complaint forms. Feedback boxes. Or how can we improve our services and suggestions tabs on their websites.

You know what I'm talking about it.

Because at one stage or another I'm sure you like myself have searched for such a place. A place to tell that café, business, restaurant, hotel, or company just how much we did not enjoy their service, or perhaps it was to express how poorly we were treated and how unprofessional and lousy their staff members were.

But have you ever used such a place to do the complete opposite? To love them?

I have. And I now do!

I remember when it first started….

It all started one day when I found myself incredibly excited about a new caramel chocolate bar. I'm talking like really REALLY excited! For those who don't know me, I absolutely adore caramel. Like (read obsessively) love caramel. It is heaven in my mouth.

Anyway, a few years ago, I cut out all dairy products from my diet. Already a vegetarian, I was slowly trying to eat less and less animalrelated products such as dairy. And on top of this I decided to cut out sugar!

A hard feat when I love caramel, chocolate, and all things dairy filled and sweet!

However, not long after I cut down on my sugars and completely cut dairy from my diet, I discovered the most amazing raw vegan chocolate bars. I'm talking super-duper absolutely to die for heaven in your mouth chocolate bars.

They are incredible but then one day it happened. The unthinkable!

I discovered they had a caramel one. And my life changed forever.

No way had I ever thought it was possible. Caramel!? I had long since said goodbye to my sweet dear friend the caramel, thinking I would never again eat such a thing. As caramel without dairy and sugar, well… is it even possible?

Well it is! And it even comes in one great big giant chocolate block!

The caramel is made from cashew nuts, coconut nectar and cacao butter, and lots of other yummy and good for you ingredients. And honestly, it's seriously divine.

I loved it so much I had to tell the company. Immediately. I wanted to love them in some way, thanking them and returning to them the love these bars were now giving me.

So I decided to do so the only way I knew how - contact them.

However I had a problem.

There was no contact number, email address, or any other way to contact them via their website. All I could seem to find was a Return and Complaints form, neither of which I wanted to do.

I certainly wasn't returning my caramel bar and a complaint was far from what I was experiencing!

I was left with two choices. One, don't contact them. Or two, love them and find a way to contact them anyway. I was contacting them!

So do you know what I did?

I used the complaint forms. Yep! I downloaded the return and or complaints form and started to write.

I don't need to go into too much detail here as to what I wrote, as you can probably get the general idea of what was written. Basically the complaints form was filled with not one single word of complaint but instead lots of praise, loads of love, and mountains upon mountains of gratitude.

I never did hear back from them.

And you know what, I was ok with that. Because I honestly did not send the form to get a thank you or reply in return. I sent it because I wanted to love them and express my love. I was being love. And when you are being love you are doing so because you want to, not because you expect anything back.

However I did get something back that day. A new secret little love revolution of mine - to contact companies and love them via their complaint forms!

I would never have thought of doing such a thing had I not been in a situation where I was so determined to choose and be love I had no choice. And I love that.

Love is always possible, even when it may seem impossible. And I assure you, even when it appears it isn't, there will always be a way to love. Because when you are powered up with love in your heart, a complaints only, no contact number available, or some other huge block in the way will never stop you.

Love doesn't give up and it certainly never fails. Love simply just is. And will always, always, find a way. The question is - will you let it?

Practice:

Today look for a service you experienced recently. Maybe it was a great meal you had at your favourite café, the bookstore you love, or even the person who served you within this service.

Can you thank them today?

Can you go online, call their boss or management? Perhaps you could thank them via email or give them a positive review on one of the many reviewing websites?

Whatever you decide to do, make it sincere, make it honest, and fill it with love.

My Son's Homework

By now you have probably guessed how much I love being love by using words and appreciation. I'ts one of my favorite ways to love, right up there along with surprise gift giving!

One of the reasons I love expressing love with words is how many ways you can do it. Notes, letters, poems, songs. It's endless!

And once you start love bombing with words, you'll be amazed at how many opportunities there are to do so.

In the following, I share with you all about a time I love bombed my son's homework.

All three of my sons bring home homework. They hate it, and at times I'm often with them. It's such an effort - on both parts, theirs and mine!

Yet it has to be done, so we do it. Each set of homework has a section at the bottom for the parents to complete if they choose. A space where we can add comments or a little note on how they went with their homework, and what struggles they may have experienced.

I usually leave this section blank and sign where required. Unless something during the week had raised concerns, like the one week I remember writing a lengthy essay on why this week's homework was way too much homework for any seven year old to undertake and complete in one week. I admit I'm still a little embarrassed by this outburst. But then, one day I decided to write something a little different. Something which the section is not used for – love.

I wrote,

"Julian, my son, is amazing. I am so proud of him and the work he is doing. I love him, and I love and thank you too Mrs. Brown, for taking care of and teaching my beautiful boy everyday. May you both be blessed today xox"
I had love bombed it.
Right there in the middle of my son's homework.
Not entirely what the comment's section is meant for, but still, everything I wrote was true.
To think such a little act of love and a few mere words could bring love into another's day (and in my case, a young overworked teacher's day) is enough to make me want to love bomb all the time!
Being love. It's simple. It really is and there are opportunities everywhere. But do we see them? And more importantly when we do, do we use them?

Practice:

Look for an opportunity to love bomb someone today.
You could hide a note in a place you know it will be found. At work, in public restroom, inside a library book, in a friend's coat pocket, on a mirror, or even randomly post a love bomb note to someone you hardly know at all or don't know!
The choice is yours. Keep it simple. Fill the note with love and bomb it.

Eat Grapes. Bop Your Head. Be Happy

I want to end it here on how simple it really is to be love, and how 'being' love really isn't doing or being anything at all. It just is!

I've never seen love be more simple and expressed more purely than in babies. They are twenty four seven, always, and in every moment, being love.

Watch them. See how easy it is. And like my son in the following story even something as basic as eating a grape can be done in love and with so much joy!

Oh to be that way again. Living every day as love and loving every day you live. Loving in whatever way you can,. whether that be with words, actions, or simply bopping your head in pure delight.

Young children do it, babies do it. So why can't we? No one ever said it had to stop…

How great are grapes!

Such little bundles of juicy goodness!

I remember it was my youngest son Gabe who had the biggest love for them.

Every time I would give him a bowl of grapes, I'd sit down and get ready for the spectacle that was about to begin. I could hardly wait to watch him as he ate them. Because honestly it was one of the most joyful and best things I have ever witnessed!

Gabe would pick up one grape at a time from his bowl, examine it intensely, bite it in half, raise it to his eyes, examine it some more, suck it, bite it again and then finally eat it.

I kid you not, he would continue to do this with every single individual grape that was in his bowl all while bopping his head, singing to himself and giggling.

A grape?

That much time and attention to a single grape? And the joy!!!

But they were only grapes?

And when such a simple thing like this can give so much pleasure to a young toddler, it makes you wonder why as adults we no longer find joy and pleasure in the simple things? And instead require much bigger things.

What would happen if we all started choosing love every day?

Deciding to love everything extravagantly which brings us joy, expressing it to the world boldly, and dismissing everything that doesn't?

I say let's all celebrate and love life the way my son eats grapes. Savoring each and every little bit, bopping your head in joy as you do, and then sharing it with others.

Simple as that.

Practice:

Find yourself today doing something you enjoy and instead of just 'enjoying' it - go all out. Celebrate it, go wild with your celebration and joy!

An example could be when going for a walk you enjoy instead of just walking and enjoying the walk, dance a little, sing a little, add a little 'bop' to your step.

Or perhaps you enjoy making cakes and cooking. Can you amp up the level of joy here in it anyway? Perhaps singing loudly as you do or even filming yourself and sharing with a friend?

Whatever it is you do that brings you joy, do more of it and do it with as much love as you possibly can. Because this is your life and yours daily to choose to live and choose to love.

So what will you choose?

To You The Reader

This isn't the end! Ok, it actually is the end of the book. But it isn't the end of my crazy walk with love, its stories, and adventures. I'm still doing those and will continue to love the path I walk daily, looking for more and more ways to love my life and more ways to commit acts of love and see it in others.

So if you like what you've read here and want more then head on over to my Facebook page where you can join me, and many others, who are choosing to love every day.

I'd love to hear from you and how you love, been loved, or will love. Either way in whatever way love was expressed, received, given, or felt, please share it. Because love shared is love given, and so many others would love to hear all about it.

Until my next book.

Be the love the world needs today.

Yours always.
Nicole x
See Love. Choose Love. Be Love.

Lightning Source UK Ltd.
Milton Keynes UK
UKHW052120290422
402296UK00011B/144